Crappy
to
Happy

Other Books by Rev. Ariel Patricia

Chaos to Clarity: Sacred Stories of Transformational Change
God is in the Little Things: Messages from the Animals
God is in the Little Things: Messages from the Golden Angels
Scanning for Signal (Co-Author)

Other Books by Kathleen O'Keefe-Kanavos

Chaos to Clarity: Sacred Stories of Transformational Change
Dreams That Can Save Your Life: Early Warning Signs of Cancer and Other Diseases (Co-Author)
Surviving Cancerland: Intuitive Aspects of Healing

Sacred Stories of Transformational Joy

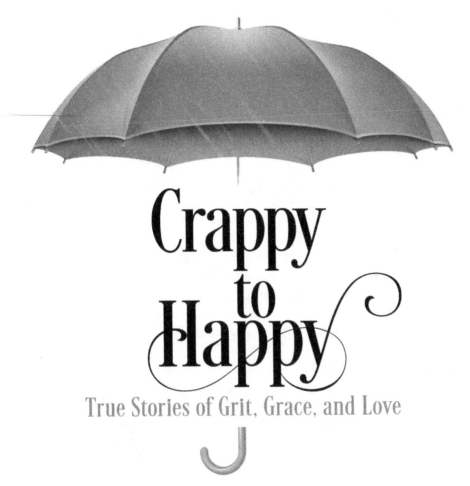

Crappy to Happy

True Stories of Grit, Grace, and Love

Rev. Ariel Patricia & Kathleen O'Keefe-Kanavos

Sacred Stories
PUBLISHING

Crappy to Happy: Sacred Stories of Transformational Joy
Rev. Ariel Patricia and Kathleen O'Keefe-Kanavos

Tradepaper ISBN: 978-1-945026-70-6
Electronic ISBN: 978-1-945026-71-3

Library of Congress Control Number: 2020943125

Published by Sacred Stories Publishing, Fort Lauderdale, FL USA

It's the same party and we're all invited.
So, can we just start dancing already?

TABLE OF CONTENTS

ACKNOWLEDGMENTS

This second book in the *Sacred Stories of Transformation* series has been a collaboration on many levels. I wish to thank Rev. Ariel Patricia of Sacred Stories Publishing for her constant inspiration and desire to continue working on making this series a success. This literary pursuit has been a challenging and joyful learning experience.

A special *thank you* to all our authors, some of whom have returned from book one, *Chaos to Clarity: Sacred Stories of Transformational Change*, to share more amazing stories. Your desire to contribute to book two is a huge compliment to us. Your stories written from the heart have brought the book to life.

To my devoted husband of almost forty years, all I can say is thank you for your endless support and understanding during the birthing of the second book *Crappy to Happy: Sacred Stories of Transformational Joy*. I love you.

-Kathleen O'Keefe-Kanavos

Thank you to my co-author Kat for continuing our collaboration and co-creating *Crappy to Happy* with me. The stories of our shared human experience are important and deserve to be told.

Thank you to our contributing authors for writing from their hearts and sharing their most intimate stories in the spirit of giving love and support to another soul living a similar experience.

And finally, a shout-out to my fellow joy chasers... you know who you are. Thank you for having the audacity and determination to keep going, even when it wasn't fun. I hope reading our book will help you shift from chasing joy to becoming joyful.

-Rev. Ariel Patricia

FOREWORD
by James Redfield

This book is enlightened — and not because it advocates some heady new theory or movement, but precisely because it doesn't!

In fact, this work transcends quick fixes and pop psychology to focus on something else: how to live life fully and spiritually in the real world of pain, self-discovery, struggle, and joy. And remarkably, what is displayed in this anthology is an authentic look at how and why joy can win.

This is a point of view much needed in today's world. Humanity continues to awaken from a materialistic sleep where spirituality has been abstracted and made theoretical, lost in an effort to solve social problems with intellectually structured platitudes about how the world might improve — leaving us to individually cope with the real challenges of life all alone.

Yet, books like this one help us face the challenges of life in a more open way, pushed along by the rising generation of Millennials, as they gain more influence. If the parents of the Millennial generation, the Baby Boomers, have been outward looking, intellectually oriented, and seeking to resolve the broad issues in human culture — minority rights, environmental protection, equal opportunity and more — Millennials naturally seem to be leading us in another, more existential direction.

Keep in mind, Millennials and their children are already the majority population on the planet. As a group they are moving well into their later thirties, the time when every generation begins to ask the larger questions in life. They seem to be asking, "I've established a way to earn money, managed to maintain key relationships, struggled to raise children. But is this all there is? What do I really want to do with my life? Does spirituality help?" The range of Millennial influence will only increase as they become even more of the majority over time, especially if the increasing number of minds thinking the same way changes us all through a kind of cultural contagion. Soul-wise, we might all be Millennials now.

The contemporary issues we face are making our culture more spiritual and more practical at the same time. The pandemic shutdown has only reinforced this openness, spawning a new sense of spiritual consciousness centered on our down-to-earth lives and how we really feel. We have already seen an explosion in personal meditation. At no other time has there been so many people practicing prayer/contemplation in the world, and that is almost entirely because of Millennial influence.

Their — our — message seems to be this: "It is time to find deeper answers about handling life! Why are we really here? How can we be happy? We have to get out of our heads, stop pretending. Give us something that acknowledges how to overcome, to break through, to open our hearts and really help each other. If the key is spiritual consciousness, show us how it applies to our everyday existence. And please can we be real?"

Again, when these are the larger questions, it doesn't take long for all of us to feel this same imperative. Suddenly, it becomes the culture's reigning sensibility, the call of the day. We want to reassess life overall, from closer to home, and with more compassion.

This enlightened book in your hands responds to this request. The contributors cover most everything from relationships to health, grief and loss, and the secrets to living an inspired journey through it all, sustained by an increase in this otherwise elusive state of joy.

Its pages take us deeply into the issues we all face, just like our newfound awareness wants. It doesn't sugarcoat problems, but it does offer grounded solutions. What is it? The "art of the comeback."

We all meet challenges when pursuing our dreams. We all get hurt. But we can also find a way to return to a joy that sustains us. It is a mysterious joy they point to, the kind that includes a peace that surpasses all understanding, as the ancient scriptures promise — a joy that, when we get knocked out of it, can be regained.

For all the pragmatic solutions that the authors and contributors realistically recommend, their auras point solidly to the larger picture emerging: Life can be lived in a new way that we can already sense, a kind of practical illumination, where we prove to ourselves that the world we live in has a spiritual design.

This book is a seminar about this emerging truth. When the heart is opened through prayer/meditation, the wounded chatter of our thoughts and emotions can be let go of, revealing a love-based, heart-opening joy and mystical peace. This peace can go farther still, of course, into a flow of intuitive intelligence and synchronicity that guides us to when and how to give miraculous help to others. That is the key to "coming back."

Such helping always leads to an awareness of the real karmic structure of life. If we help others, we will draw into our lives people who come to help us, who present us with a miracle synchronicity. And that's the secret. When we are at our lowest, if we find someone else who is down and seek to lift them up, that energy flows though us first, lifting us as well, as it extends to the other person. And all this happens at a down to earth level.

The rewards can increase, of course. When we open our hearts ever wider, this intuitive intelligence does something even more profound.

Over time, it reveals our soul's true mission and how to fulfill it, even offering intuitions of protection along the way, if we tune in.

We are not yet there perhaps. We all still stumble. But the personal stories in this book show us how to always "come back" to this path, to the illumined journey.

...I told you it was enlightened.

The Spirituality of Joy

by Rev. Ariel Patricia

Joy is in the sweetness.

Just beyond the physicality of the emotion… there is a sweetness. Oh, what a place to be—in the sweetness.

Confessions of a joy chaser.

There it is. I said it. I was a *joy chaser*… Struggling for years to feel joy in my life, I chased one experience and teaching after another. I thought if I could just go further, dive deeper, try harder that I could break through an invisible barrier that was keeping me from the life that awaited me, and I would *finally* feel joy.

The warrior in me was unsettled. She knew she could do this. She had fought tougher battles before. She thought if she pushed hard enough, she could make it happen. That's how we did things. We controlled them. We worked hard to achieve our goals and we didn't quit until we had won.

"We could go on that new spiritual journey or take more classes," my warrior whispered in my ear. "How hard could feeling joy be?"

"Yes! Of course, we can do this!" I would affirm, signing up for another course or excursion that promised me all that my heart yearned for.

In a few short years of being a joy chaser, I had exhausted myself and much of my finances and still did not understand what joy really was.

Joy is a vibration.

"What does that mean?" questioned my logical self.

"A vibration? That just sounds silly," my protector persona replied. "Don't worry about that. You're doing just fine."

"Wait! How do we create a vibration?" piped in my warrior self, excited for a goal, regardless of how nebulous, and sure she could make it happen.

"A vibration is energy, a frequency," my intellectual self proudly stated, happy to have something to show for the countless courses she had taken.

"Well, how do we create it?" my warrior pushed.

"I have no idea," replied my intellectual self, silently berating herself for not having the answer.

I want to break open with emotion.

My angst continued. I didn't have the answer, and my body felt that painful truth. My chest hurt... a lot. It wasn't a heart attack; it felt more like the bones in my chest were about to split open. Trying to capture my longing, this poem spilled out.

I want to know my soul.
To feel my connection to the birds.
To infinitely live in the sunrise and sunset of each new day.
I want to break open with emotion.
For love to permeate every fiber of my being.
To fully express the ache in my chest and the lump in my throat.
I want to breathe the air of my ancestors.

To be in communion with all that is.
For the salt from my tears to clear the mist shrouding my ability to see.
I want to remember.
I want to know my soul.

Yes, that was it. That was what I wanted. Finally, I was able to express what I was searching for.

But was it *joy*?

I wasn't sure. Reading it over, a realization struck me. My yearning was for *connection*. To be deeply connected to something greater than the physical world I was living in. "To be in communion with all that is."

Reflecting more, I knew if I wanted "to infinitely live in the sunrise and to breathe the air of my ancestors," I would have to walk differently in this world. For this depth of connection, this communion, I would have to trust... and allow.

"*Allow?* No way!" my warrior self quickly piped up. "That's too much like the *surrendering* everyone talks about!"

"Shhh! Let's give it a chance. We've tried everything else," argued my intellectual self.

"Gentle, let's be gentle," offered my usually quiet, nurturing self.

My joy is in the sweetness.

Trusting and allowing takes practice. At least, for me it did. But I found the more I could let my warrior-self stand at ease, the deeper I could connect with and know... my soul.

Happiness is an emotion and joy is a state of being. You feel happy and you are joyful. My joy is in the sweetness. A place of contentment with what is. A deep knowing that all is well, even when it seems as if chaos swirls around us. This is where the sweetness lies.

The powerful stories of transformation in this book may, at first read, not seem joyful. Some may seem downright heartbreaking. But if you look a little closer, you will see that, between the lines of each story, the authors have come to a place of knowing. In this knowing there is insight, peace, space, breath, and ultimately, sweet joy.

Enjoy,

Ariel Patricia

The Psychology of Joy

by Kathleen (Kat) O'Keefe-Kanavos

Joy gives us the power to endure life's hardships
without becoming hardened.

Humans are fragile creatures, and it is from this point of physical, psychological, and emotional truth that we often draw on joy for strength. Joy is generated from within us and is a long term state of being while happiness is a short-lived result to external stimuli. It is through joy that we feel more alive and aligned with our emotions.

Happiness will not save us from conflict or heartbreak. In fact, new research by psychologists states we might need to cry more when we are more emotionally aligned.[1] Perhaps that is why nurse Diane Vich danced before delivering bad news to families, and Catherine Paour laughed her way through open-heart surgery. However, with joy in our life, we may laugh more quickly, which appears to chase away the dark clouds of chaos.

Research into the psychology of joy and happiness has been a lifelong pursuit for many researchers, who wonder how both play into successful problem-solving and longevity, as seen in Frank Zaccari's story about his brother's horrible car accident, which left him in a wheelchair for the rest of his life. Determination fueled with a newfound joy for life changed everything.

Joy is bigger than happiness.[2] Happiness is dependent on the accumulation of external circumstances, but joy is a state of mind that animates our being.

Joy is a state of being that transcends momentary happiness.

During my most challenging times in life, I learned that joy followed by a good laugh could take away the power of whatever was holding me prisoner.[3] Facing a dangerous boogey-man with the multiple and interchangeable names of Covid, Cancer, or Crisis made me dig deep into my survival toolbox. Laughter is a blessed weapon or tool because it is contagious, too.[4]

If you see two people laughing at a joke you didn't hear, chances are you will smile anyway--even if you don't realize it. The brain responds to the sound of laughter and prepares the facial muscles to join in the mirth. Laughter is a breath of fresh air that can clear a room of stale fear.

Hanging around someone who is a "laugher" is a sure way to catch a good case of "Joy," because laughter and joy go together like peanut and butter. And although they complement each other, they are different.

Joy and happiness can metaphorically be considered siblings, but not twins.

The science behind joy shares new discoveries in experimental psychology that offer insight into human flourishing.[5] Neuroscientist Richard Davidson, a longtime friend of Tenzin Gyatso, His Holiness the 14th Dalai Lama, is a professor of psychology and psychiatry at the University of Wisconsin–Madison as well as founder and chair of the Center for Healthy Minds. His research focuses on the neural bases of emotion and neuroplasticity. Dr. Davidson says, "One can learn happiness and compassion as skills, just as one learns to play a musical instrument or train in golf or tennis."

Based on Davidson's research, well-being, happiness, and joy are rooted in neural circuits and have four constituents.[6]

Each of these neural circuits exhibit plasticity, which means if we exercise the circuits, they will strengthen. Practicing these skills can provide change, which helps promote higher levels of well-being in our lives.

The four skills are:

Resilience: Our ability to change the way we respond to challenges

Outlook: The ability to see and savor the positive in others and situations

Attention: A focus on joy

Generosity: Generous and altruistic behavior, which activates brain circuits that are key to fostering well-being and joy.

The research found that people spend an average of 47 percent of their waking life not paying attention to what they are doing—and that an unfocused mind is seldom joyful. A modest dose of simple practices like lovingkindness might alter this circuitry.

Our brains are regularly being shaped, wittingly or unwittingly. By intentionally shaping our minds, we can take responsibility for our happiness. Like joy, sadness is often a matter of perception. Therefore, it would stand to reason that we create much of our suffering—and it would be logical to assume that we can also create our joy. It merely depends on the attitude, perspective, and reactions we bring to situations.

What is the purpose of life? Is it to get rich? I have met unhappy billionaires and happy trash collectors. The difference was not how much money they saved in life, but rather how much joy they spent.

Joy can lighten the heavy footsteps of our mortality.

We might need to tackle emotional obstacles that make joy elusive. Joy is the unleashed butterfly from the cocoon of our mind because joy begins as a state of mind that morphs into a state of being. Our soul's innate lightness of being can fly above crisis and soar on the undercurrents of chaos, because our soul has seen it all and flown through it all before.

Joy leads to a life of satisfaction and meaning. It is possible to be joyful even in the face of daily challenges of varying degrees. Joy is a state of mind we can carry with us through the morning traffic, and even through anger and grief, because joy is also a state of being over which we have control. Mind over matter really does matter.

The honest and personal stories in this book beckon you to join the authors on their resilient journeys. Their positive outlooks focus on joy, despite the adversity that leads to generosity and ultimately creates psychological well-being.

I hope that, like stories in *Chaos to Clarity*, the first book of the *Sacred Stories of Transformation* series, the psychological and emotional journeys in *Crappy to Happy* will leave you filled with joy.

The power of joy allows us to endure hardship without becoming hardened. It offers a positive perspective, which opens doors to new opportunities.

May these stories of transition from strife to joy be a blessing for all sentient beings traveling the long and winding road of life.

PART 1

LOVE AND RELATIONSHIPS
Crazy Little Thing Called Love

And I feel the call of my heart once more
And it is safe and familiar
Because I am right where
I am supposed to be

Love Between Lives
by Rev. Ariel Patricia

A deeper connection shining through.

The sanctuary space was quiet—peaceful, really—a direct contradiction to the anticipation overwhelming me. A few soft lights and many candles radiated a soothing energy and beckoned me to breathe, to relax, and slow down my racing heart. My body reflexively listened, and as a deep breath filled my lungs, I delighted in the fragrance of lavender and lemon in the air.

Needing a moment to observe, I had taken a seat in the back of the room. I quietly observed the group of people, my companions for the evening, as they got settled. They silently busied themselves: arranging their spaces, taking out their journals, finding an elusive pen to write with, and mentally preparing for the experience to come. Their looks were varied, but most were nondescript, like me—dressed in jeans and T-shirts, sweatpants and sweatshirts, comfortable clothes that would not encumber them or their experience.

Tonight, I will experience my first past-life regression.

"Welcome, everyone! Get your pillow and blanket and find a place that you feel comfortable," Maria, our leader, instructed.

Since I wasn't sure what to expect, I wanted to be as private as possible, so I found a space against the back wall. I settled in, my pillow under my head and a blanket wrapped around me, creating a cocoon. Finally, I said a silent prayer, asking my angels to support me and allow me to have the full experience.

"You will be conscious the entire time, and if anything happens that troubles you, you can just open your eyes," Maria reassured us. "Your conscious and subconscious mind will both be active. You can release any concerns and just allow the experience. You are safe and supported."

The lights dimmed further; we closed our eyes, and soft music played in the background. Maria, with a serene tone and a soothing cadence to her voice, began a meditation to help us calm our breathing and clear our minds from distracting thoughts. My heartbeat slowed down to a steady, rhythmic beat, slower and slower until my mind quieted and my conscious mind centered inward.

We were ready to begin.

I am standing on the top of a magnificent staircase, which reaches high into the breathtaking blue sky that surrounds it. The staircase is white marble, and the steps curve downward in a long, graceful sweep, connecting the sky to the earth. With one hand resting lightly on the banister, I slowly descend. As I reach the last step, a lush garden springs up around me. Colorful flowers of all varieties greet me: some large and some tall, straining their ginger and golden faces to feel the warmth of the sun, while others seem content to sprawl along the garden floor, creating a patchwork of scarlet and violet. Butterflies flit by and birds sing a chorus of melodies in the trees. As I breathe in the scents of the life all around me, a smile graces my lips.

Feeling safe and secure, I walk into my garden, my fingertips caressing the petals of the flowers as I pass. As trees start to dot the edge of my vision, a bubbling stream becomes visible at my feet. Walking along the soft earth beside the stream, I find a bench to rest on. I breathe deeply and look out over the horizon. The sun is starting to set, blazing an intense fire of color across the sky. I rest for a moment, but I know that time is getting short.

Not too far ahead, at the entrance to the forest, I see a gate that is painted white and arched at the top. The most beautiful white light is shining through the diamond-shaped openings of the latticework. Excited, I hurry forward, as I know I am to walk through the gate.

"Look down at your feet," Maria prompts. "What are you wearing?"

I look down. Very large male feet, wrapped in Roman sandals, greet my eyes. I blink and look again. With dismay, I see they are not only male feet but flat and with square toes.

What? Whose feet are these? I wonder, looking for my slender, feminine feet with toenails painted red.

I must be doing something wrong. I look down again, and again, I am greeted with the same large, flat, male feet wearing Roman sandals. I am not able to focus, and I need a moment to process this information. An odd tingling creeps up my spine.

"Where are you? Who do you see?" Maria asks the group.

Her voice brings me back. I feel strange, but in this lifetime, I am a man. Tearing my eyes away from my feet, I pick up my head and look around. I am in Roman times—I believe during the height of the Roman Empire. I am wearing a short, white toga that falls loosely to my knees, tied at the waist with a belt of some kind. I look about thirty years old and have short, light-brown hair.

People are gathered in a public square. The day is hot, and grumbles from the crowd are getting louder and more frequent. I am standing in the front of a group of men wearing togas similar to mine. Facing us is a crowd of Roman soldiers dressed in full armor with plated breastplates and helmets. The tension between my group and the soldiers is palpable, but I stand straight and hold my head high. I am fearless, and a leader to the men standing behind me.

Suddenly, before I can speak, there is a rustle in the crowd of soldiers. In a flash, an arm is raised, a body lunges forward, and a spear is thrust into my chest!

Maria is speaking again. "Leave this time and go forward in your life. Where are you now? What is happening?"

Again, I am confused. How can I go forward? Didn't I just get stabbed? Didn't I die?

I take a breath and try to clear my mind. I look around. I am not dead. Somehow, I survived, and I have recovered. I see myself resting; however, my confusion has taken up so much time that Maria is speaking again.

"Go forward again to the end of this lifetime, to your death scene. What do you see?" Maria asks.

Refocused and calm, I go forward. I am an old man lying on a decorative concrete bench on a hillside overlooking a city. It is springtime: the ground is covered in lush green grass; the heat of the summer has not yet started to take its toll, and the cool air has a dewy feel, as if it has recently rained. My home, a lavish estate, is behind me, and my wife of many years is by my side. Her long, gray, wavy hair reaches far down her back, worn loose today, with no adornments to restrain its beauty. Her hands are holding mine, and her eyes glisten with the tears she is holding back. She smiles at *me, her gentle smile that I have loved for a lifetime, as she tries to mask the pain, I know she is carrying in her heart.*

I am near death. I pull my gaze from hers and look over on the hillside, where many adult people are gathered. They are my children and their spouses. Everyone is here for me, to say their good-byes. I am growing weary, but I am not afraid, as I am surrounded by love. I am content. My life has been a good one.

Maria speaks. "It is time to return to your body now. I will start counting backwards from ten to one. Say good-bye and start walking back through the gate. When I reach the count of one, you will be back in your body, and when you are ready, you can open your eyes.

I sighed and returned. People were talking. They were sharing their experiences, but I couldn't talk yet, emotion coursing through my body.

I could still feel the love.

I had seen a happy lifetime when I lived with someone I loved very much and with whom I had a large, loving family. Two years post-divorce, and as I was just starting to feel better emotionally, I was overcome with gratitude and elated with the knowledge that I had experienced real, lasting love before. A stinging sensation pricked the corner of my eyes, and I sat in silence as my vision blurred, tears sliding down my cheeks.

We took a quick break to regroup, and Maria soon explained that it was time to do the next regression. The process would be the same as before. I felt certain that, having done one regression—and coming to terms with the knowledge that I was previously a man—I would be able to relax and embrace whatever was shown to me next.

I walk down my grand staircase, through the beautiful garden, past the stream, stepping through the gate and into the light. I look down at my feet and see tall, dressy, dark-brown boots that lace up the front and come up to about mid-calf. A long, deep-blue velvet coat with buttons up the front and a high stiff collar, the type worn in the United States in the early 1800s, keeps me warm. My hair is walnut brown, grown long, with pipe curls pulled up in the back so the curls cascade to just below my shoulders, reminiscent of hair adorning a porcelain doll, complete with a blue velvet hat capped with a feather. I am a young woman in my twenties, slender and attractive.

The clip-clopping sound of horses' hooves fills the air. As I look up, a carriage drawn by a large black horse moves slowly past. I am standing on a sidewalk in what I believe to be Boston, MA. A narrow, cobblestoned street is before me, winding through the city's tightly packed brick buildings. On the brown brick building across the street, an address marker catches my eye, and I know that is where I am going.

The baby in my arms starts to squirm, and my attention is diverted to my children. In addition to my baby, two young children, a boy and a girl, around four or five years of age, are with me. They are not twins but are close in age. My son looks handsome in matching shorts and jacket. His fists are clenched, elbows bent, and a wide smile crosses his young face as he jumps with great zeal next to me, the way only little boys seem to do. My daughter looks very much like a little lady, dressed in a button-up coat similar to mine. Waiting patiently, she holds tightly onto my coat, her behavior much different than her active brother's. We are preparing to cross the street. I call my son to my side and remind them to hold on to my coat as we cross. Smiling, I take a step, a young mother happy and busy with my young children.

Maria's voice interrupts my memory, and she asks us to move forward in this life. I take a deep breath and see myself lying on a twin-sized bed. The room is small and dark, lit only by an oil lamp on a side table and the last remnants of the sun's rays coming through the lone window. Hot and uncomfortable, my sweat is sticking my long, loose hair to my face. I scream out, and a woman comes to my side. It is time.

I am in the final stages of labor and just about to give birth. My body writhes with pain as the midwife holds a cold cloth to my forehead, encouraging me with her words. The baby is coming, and with a final push, I witness the birth of my son. I am exhausted by the birth, but happy. The midwife wraps my son in a blanket and lays him in my arms. As I lie there welcoming my child, she asks me if I would like to see my husband.

"Of course!" I respond, eager to see him.

She hurries to get him. He has been waiting in the next room, and he quickly comes in. Taking my hand, he sits down by my side, and I look up at him, excited to share the birth with him. Looking into his eyes, I see into his soul, and I am not prepared for what I see. The eyes that are staring back into mine are those of my ex-husband, Steve.

What? my mind reacts.

I don't want it to be Steve! I am upset, disappointed. How could it be Steve, the man that I am now divorced from, the man that did not love me enough to stay and try to work things out? Shaken, I try to come to terms with this. I look again into the eyes of my husband, who is so lovingly sitting by my side, hoping for a different response.

Yes, it is most certainly Steve.

Maria's voice cuts through my thoughts, the haze of my disappointment. She asks us to go forward to our death in this life. I take a deep breath and *try to move forward, no longer interested in learning anything more. I am completely shaken by the fact that my husband in my former life is my ex-husband in this life.*

After a moment, with little enthusiasm, I move to my death scene. It is early morning, and I wake to the sweet smell of the honeysuckle vines by my window, still fragrant with the morning dew. My body aches, and it is difficult to get out of bed. I am content to lie here for a few more minutes, as I am feeling extremely tired, and it is so early that I have yet to hear the birds' morning songs.

Rubbing the soreness from my hands, I am taken with my gnarled fingers and bulging, blue veins; gone is the smooth, unblemished skin of a younger woman. The tiredness begins to worsen and weigh on me like a heavy cloak. My eyelids are heavy, and I close my eyes, unaware that it is for the last time.

"It is time to return to your bodies," Maria says in her soothing voice. "I will count down from ten to one. When I reach one, you need to return through the gate and back into your body."

Maria begins to count. I am not paying attention. I see something off in the distance, a golden light.

What is that light? *I move toward it.*

"Nine ... eight ... start to come back." Maria is counting.

I ignore her and move in the direction of the light. I am getting closer. I have to see what it is. "Seven ... six ..."

It looks like a person! I can't turn away. I am being inexplicably drawn forward. I continue toward the light.

The man in the distance is standing tall and straight; his broad shoulders are thrust back, his head held high, and his legs parted but ramrod straight.

A golden light is emanating from him and luminously radiating all around him. His strength and power are palpable. My excitement builds, and I continue forward. I can now see his wings, expansive and brilliant golden wings. He is an angel! He holds a long sword, pointed downward, in front of him. His stance and presence are powerful, but inviting, and I know there is no danger.

"Five ... four ..."

I keep going forward, like a moth drawn to a light. My breath catches as more golden beings begin to appear. On each side of him, one at a time, alternating left and right, golden beings appear. It is reminiscent of a panel of people standing on a dais. I feel that they are there to greet me, to welcome me. There is a familiarity to them, and I believe that I know them, but I am not close enough yet to see their faces.

"Three ... two ... you're almost to the gate. At one, you will go through the gate and back into your body."

No! I don't want to go back. I want to go toward the golden beings. Every cell of my body is reaching toward them. I need to clearly see their faces! I want to talk to them! There is such a love and a warmth emanating from them that it makes me ache.

"One."

Pop! I go back, through the gate and into my body. I feel jarred by the suddenness, filled with disappointment, and left with a deep longing. This was not where I wanted to be. I wanted to be with the golden beings.

Numbness and confusion enveloped me. People were talking, but I was not paying attention. Questions were running through my head. *Why didn't I have more time? Why couldn't I get closer?* and most importantly, *who are they?*

I must ask Maria for an explanation. At the first opportunity, I raised my hand and relayed what had just happened. What Maria said next shocked me.

"Sometimes during a regression, when we come to the end of a life, our soul wants to go forward to its soul state and not go back into the body. Your soul was being called forward. In between our physical lives, there is a spiritual realm we return to. This is where we meet with our guides and reflect on our experiences in the physical state. It is there that we decide what the next step for our soul will be. This time is referred to as 'life between lives,' and the golden beings that you saw were either your soul family or your guides."

Yes, instinct told me she was right. I could *feel* the pull toward the golden light; it was familiar and welcoming. I knew I was supposed to go back to the gate and into my body, but I didn't care. I had to move toward the light. To me, this confirmed that we are so much more than our physical form.

I lay there, wrapped in my blanket; my muscles released their tension, and as my head rested lightly on my pillow, a comforting warmth permeated my body and an unexpected smile found its way onto my lips. I had much to contemplate, to process. I thought of my wife from Roman times as she gazed at me with a deep love in her eyes, and I knew that I had felt true and lasting love, which was a welcome balm to my raw and still-bleeding heart. My husband from Boston—although it had initially upset me to recognize my ex-husband, Steve—confirmed for me a deeper connection shining through, a recognition of my soul seeing an old friend. My golden angels, the beings from whom I felt such a profound pull... I now knew I was connected to and guided by them. That was enough.

I reveled in the fact that, in one evening, I had received absolute confirmation that we are not alone. I had been shown that we not only travel through lives with other spiritual friends, but we are fully supported and guided by loving beings, such as my golden angels. My eyes filled with tears as this truth permeated my human shell and settled deep within my soul. The pain and the loneliness that had threatened to suffocate me since the divorce was finally being released.

My Child Was Still My Child
by Lorilyn Rizzo Bridges

Our love for each other saved us.

The phone call came as my husband Peter and I were preparing for a two-week trip to Sicily to explore my ancestry. It was my oldest child, Teddy. I immediately sensed something was wrong. Really wrong.

Teddy was a couple of weeks shy of turning twenty-nine and lived more than 3,000 miles away in Los Angeles, but we spoke frequently. We've always been extremely close, especially when Teddy teetered on the brink of national stardom in the music industry back in the early 2000s, and since choosing a music career behind the scenes.

Lately, Teddy had been experiencing tremendous success professionally, but physically had been struggling with some serious issues; stomach pain, bouts of nausea and anxiety. I was disappointed and concerned to learn Teddy had taken to smoking copious amounts of weed and cigarettes to cope. It clearly wasn't helping. His health issues were only getting worse.

"Hey, Momma..."

Teddy's voice sounded small and sullen.

All it took was those two words.

I could tell that Teddy had finally hit a wall. In those two words, I could hear pain, despair, frustration and—worst of all—a lack of hope.

Call it a mother's intuition, but I knew if I left for Sicily, I'd be coming home to a nightmare. I decided on the spot to postpone our trip until there was a specific plan in place. I contacted "Teddy's Team," and they, Teddy, and I worked to find a program and a facility where Teddy could finally address these issues.

Feeling Teddy was in good hands, my husband and I left for Palermo. We explored the countryside and thoroughly enjoyed ourselves. Three days before the end of our trip, I was eager to return to our villa, because it was the first time in two weeks Teddy was able to take phone calls.

As my husband perused the travel guide to find a restaurant for dinner, I grabbed my cell phone and headed to the enormous baroque parlor, where I flopped down on the sofa.

I had a million questions: *How was the facility? What were the programs like? And most importantly: How was it going with addressing "those issues?"*

"Hey Bud!" I exclaimed. "It's so good to hear your voice! How are you?"

"I'm good, Momma… really good…. How's Sicily?"

There was something in Teddy's voice that made me take pause.

"I'm… good…" I replied, while my *momma mind* was busy trying to access what was worrying me.

Silence.

"Mom?" Teddy had sensed my voice trail off in thought.

"Yep! I'm here, Bud."

"Hey Mom, I need to tell you something."

My mind swirled. What could it be? Teddy sounded more clear-headed than I'd heard in years, no longer numb from the weed. So, what was the news?

"Mom?" Teddy's strong, calm, confident voice interrupted my thoughts.

"Yes?" I heard myself say.

Teddy inhaled deeply. "Mom, I …"

Have you ever thought about your very first memory?

Don't ask me why, but right then, at that very instant, I had a flashback. I was sitting in my crib crying… I mean, I was exhausted from crying. I was cold, wet, and hungry.

It's a memory, but it's actually more like an all-encompassing feeling… a feeling of being alone… scared… vulnerable.

It was a feeling I'd tried to suppress most of my life… a memory I feared remembering. Because most of my childhood felt this way. The word "childhood" suggests a pleasant, carefree time when one is raised by their parents, but that couldn't have been further from my truth. Honestly, if anyone raised me… it was my older sister.

You see, I was born to a severely phobic, clinically depressed mother and a father who battled multiple addictions. My world was broken. We can summarize my "childhood" by comparing it to being on a jumbo jet where the pilot and co-pilot were both passed out cold.

I spent a lot of time daydreaming, imagining how I could fix my world. I dreamed about how wonderful my life was going to be when I was a grown-up. I dreamed of being the best wife and mother in the world. I wanted to have a ton of kids and a dog, and live happily-ever-after in a big old farmhouse. I'd make quilts, bake cookies, and plant vegetables and flowers. Most of all, I was determined that my own children would have a magical childhood.

I was going to do everything differently from my parents. So, when I met a guy in college who seemed to be the opposite of my father, I married him. He was twenty-two, I was twenty-three, and I naively ignored every bright red flag that warned this was not the right man for me.

My head convinced my heart I was doing the right thing. But, by the time I wondered if I'd made a big mistake... I'd delivered a beautiful baby boy named Teddy.

Life is funny.

After all those years daydreaming about being the most perfect wife and mother, I had become Martha Stewart *and* Mrs. Brady on steroids.

I had Teddy, then another baby boy, then a baby girl... and I was so busy working hard to make everything perfect, I hardly noticed my world was broken once again.

No matter how hard I worked to fix everything, my marriage was unraveling, and my children's father was barely there for them physically or emotionally.

After twenty-three years of marriage, he asked for a divorce. What followed was a nightmare. It was a high-conflict Family Court struggle worse than anything you could imagine.

Once it was settled, my kids and I began to heal, and eventually little miracles began to happen. I reconnected with an old friend named Peter who I'd known since high school. We shared how our personal lives had turned out very differently than we'd hoped and we realized we had much more in common than our failed first marriages.

After a four-year courtship, Peter and I married. It felt like everything was finally falling into place for everyone.

Everyone, except maybe Teddy.

As I sat in Sicily clutching my cell phone tightly, I knew something was up and that Teddy was about to tell me something important. I tried to push those old memories of feeling alone and scared and vulnerable from my mind. I held my breath as Teddy inhaled deeply…

"Mom, I… have always believed … and felt … *and known*, I am a woman.

I said nothing.

"Mom. I. Am. A. Woman."

Complete silence.

"Mom?"

No air in the room or in my lungs.

"Mom?"

My mind raced, thinking, *Oh God, please don't say 'Mom' again because I can't answer… I want to… I want to say whatever it is you need to hear right now… but I can't say a word.*

I felt like I had been pushed onstage in a play, but I didn't know the lines.

I finally manage to say one tiny word, spoken like a broken whisper. "Okay."

I didn't even know if I had meant to phrase it as a question or a statement. It felt as if someone else had said it.

What. The. Heck!

Time stood still… I'm not sure for how long.

It was midday, but suddenly, the parlor was as dark as midnight and there I was, sitting alone on the sofa. Those old memories engulfed me once again. My world felt like it had broken wide open.

Finally, I spoke again: "Okay. I'm just not sure what to say, Honey. I had no idea. I had no idea you *ever* felt this way…"

"I know." Teddy replied. "I made sure you never knew."

How could I have not known? It was my job to know everything about my kids, to anticipate what they needed before they even knew. I was a horrible mother, even worse than I feared. *How did I miss this?*

"Teddy, when did you start to feel this way?"

"As far back as I can remember… definitely around age five. I've always felt this way, Mom. I just never gave it much thought. When I was young, I just figured everyone felt the same way. And then when I realized other people didn't feel the same way I did, I felt ashamed and just kept quiet about it. I never thought there was anything I could do about it. So, I just dealt with my feelings privately. I would explore what made me feel normal and comfortable only in private… I never wanted anyone to know…. I was *terrified* someone would find out."

Suddenly, I felt terrified. I'd seen movies about kids living with these deep, dark secrets and the horrible side effects caused by all the buried fear and shame. Addiction, anxiety, depression, behavioral issues … even suicide!

Teddy had been dealing with this all alone. Anything could have happened. At that moment, I felt overwhelmingly grateful. My child, at the age of twenty-nine, finally felt able to open up.

Time... a safe setting... and skilled therapy had all helped to pull back the layers that had numbed his reality for so long.

I no longer cared about the years lost or the decades it took for Teddy to finally feel safe enough to share. What mattered was that we were given a second chance.

"Mom, I love you. I know this is a lot to take in right now, but one of the group sessions is starting and I have to go. We'll talk more when you get back to the states... okay?"

"Okay," I answered. "No problem, Honey."

"Okay, great. I'll talk to you in a couple days."

"Hey Teddy — I love you, Bud. *I love you so much.* And listen to me. This is all going to be okay. No worries, all right?" I said, reassuring myself more than Teddy.

"I know, Mom. I love you. Bye, Momma."

I had no idea what to expect.

I don't know how long I sat there with my silent cellphone in my hand. I was scared and confused, but also grateful and terrified, all at once.

Eventually, Peter came into the room. I could hear him asking me, "How's Teddy doing?"

I looked up but couldn't answer.

I. Could. Not. Speak.

Never in my life had I been completely speechless, until that moment.

Eventually, I simply said, "Teddy is a woman."

And just like that my life changed in an instant. And once again my world broke wide open.

When I returned from Sicily, reality hit.

Late one night, I felt an overwhelming sense of dread, loss, worry, guilt, and grief. That night, I wept inconsolably for the past and for the future. I wept for the end of a reality I'd known since the day Teddy was born.

I wept for Teddy, for my younger two kids, for my parents, and for myself. And when there were no tears left to cry, I dried my eyes and took a deep breath.

There was no point in looking back. It was time to move forward, to heal our world—but how?

I knew nothing about the transitioning process my child was about to begin. So, I did what everyone does: I turned to the internet, googled "*transgender*," and went from there.

I ended up handwriting seven pages of definitions for words I'd never heard before. I watched a bunch of fascinating and enlightening Ted Talks. I'd never met a transgender person (that I knew of), and it was reassuring to learn they were just regular, everyday folks. I found a therapist who worked with families (especially moms) going through this type of enormous change. I also discovered Facebook groups and connected with local organizations and support groups.

There was plenty of new information to take in and understand. But there was one thing I knew with 100 percent certainty….

Teddy was still Teddy—the same heart, same soul, same spirit.

I knew my child was still my child.

The only thing that had changed was that Teddy had made a decision to finally transition into living her authentic life. With the help of qualified medical professionals and counselors, she would make the necessary changes to finally align her outward expression of gender to match her authentic gender.

Of course, transitioning to a woman would affect not only Teddy, but our whole family. For thirty years, Teddy's family had only known her as male. This, I believe, is what causes the greatest conflict for families. We need time to catch up to understanding this reality, which is new to us but not to the person transitioning.

Teddy asked me to tell her brother and sister. They were both tremendously supportive.

I had no idea how the rest of the family would handle this information, knowing everyone processes things in their own way and in their own time. Once again, I was grateful for the depth of love and support our family showed Teddy.

Growing up is not easy. Parenting is not easy. Life is not easy.

Sometimes, our world can break wide open and things can feel pretty crappy.

But we gain our strength and equilibrium from the love and support of those around us. Therefore, it is up to all of us to cultivate a supportive environment of kindness, inclusivity, and—most of all—faith, hope, and love.

Idle Gatherings
by Janet Cincotta

The moment you speak the truth, the cheering gets louder.

Every so often, my best friend Kate and I indulge in a relaxing meal at our favorite restaurant. We let somebody else set the table and we linger over a meal we didn't have to prepare, leaving the cleanup to the kitchen crew.

I think my husband hates these dinners, as he imagines the two of us dissecting his brain by candlelight, right there in the middle of the restaurant. I'm a doctor and Kate is a nurse, so we could do it.

The truth is, we do sometimes speculate about the workings of his mind, as well as a few other parts of his anatomy, but there's more to it than that. When we get together like this, we like to brag about our dogs and our grandchildren. We find things to laugh about that no one else considers funny. And sometimes, we quilt. We gather up the tattered scraps of our lives—the bright bits of hope and happiness, the faded snippets of sorrow and worry, the ragged fabric of disappointment and despair—and between courses, we stitch them together again. And that takes time.

So, it wasn't because we'd wolfed down our meal that night, nor was it because the service was especially snappy—but when our plates were empty and our waiter rushed in to clear the table, we were not ready to say good-bye. We had finished the evening's dissection and patched up our lives, but we hadn't even touched on world hunger, social injustice, or the sad state of our teeth, hair, and nails. We still had work to do.

When our waiter appeared with the check, Kate waved him away.

Then, just as quickly, she called him back. Normally, she shuns dessert, and she rarely drinks coffee—so when she ordered one of those thick, warm brownies topped with ice cream, chocolate syrup, and whipped cream, accompanied by a mug of strong black coffee, I knew something was on her mind. Something that called for comfort food and caffeine.

I ordered another glass of good red wine.

When her dessert arrived, Kate pushed her plate toward me. "Here," she said. "Let's split this."

This is the definition of a friend: a person who offers to share comfort food with you when she's about to deliver bad news. Someone who spots the ticking bomb in your life, warns you about it before it can detonate, and sticks around for the aftermath, to make sure you survive.

A true friend carries emergency supplies wherever she goes. In case there's blood.

The conversation went something like this:

"No, thanks," I said. "So, what's on your mind?"

"What do you mean, what's on my mind?"

"Dessert? And coffee? At nine o'clock? Something's up," I insisted.

"Okay," she said. "You're right. It's just that I've been wondering about something. Do you think your husband would ever have an affair?"

Well, sure enough, that took me by surprise—although, truth be told, I'd been wondering about it myself. I'd watched my closest friends go through it, so I knew the signs. The distance between the couples grew, and the silence deepened. Disbelief morphed into denial, and denial dissolved into heartache. And then, divorce finished them off.

Divorce would have come as no surprise to me. I'd been toying with the idea myself, praying about it as if it were acceptable to pray for help with a mortal sin, to pray that my husband would commit it and let me off the hook. *"Please, Lord, let him be man enough to go. Let him leave a note on the kitchen table, empty his closet, and make off with the hard drive and power tools. Let him be the one who breaks the covenant of our marriage and forsakes his children."*

If only he would be a man about it, I thought, I could immerse myself in self-pity and bask in the warm glow of righteous indignation. I'd already contemplated all the delicious ways I could console myself after he left. Perhaps a new wardrobe would help. Or a cruise. Or a new puppy.

It would be just like him to brood over it in silence, work out every detail without a word, and then, when everything was just the way he wanted it, to drop it in my lap right at the kitchen table. All while pretending nothing was wrong.

I'd already erected an emotional barricade around the man.

I allowed him work without interruption, to come and go without a word. I vowed to keep whatever troubles I had to myself, to take on the intrusions and distractions of our existence without a fuss. I didn't nag him for help around the house. I didn't ask him what he wanted for dinner, or what he thought we should get his sister for her birthday, or what color I should paint the bathroom. I didn't bother him when I was lonely or bored or sad or worried. I'd already learned to live without him.

Still, we are devout Catholics, and in the Church, marriage is considered a sacrament. Irrevocable. Eternal. There's a lot of pressure to make it work. And my husband was a respected leader in the community, a man known for his self-discipline, honesty, and integrity. I didn't think he would stoop to divorce. If I was willing to tough it out, I figured he should be, too.

"No," I said. "I don't think he would."

Kate hesitated as though trying to decide if I could handle the truth. She brushed some crumbs off the table and watched them fall to the floor

"Well, he is," she said. "He has been for a while."

Bam! There it was. The other shoe had dropped.

She proceeded to fill me in on the details. Who he was seeing, how long it had been going on, who else knew about it, and where my husband and his girlfriend had been spotted together. She shared an office with him, so she knew the truth, and like the brave friend she was, she spoke it.

This took a while to sink in, but it made sense.

It explained where he was all those nights when I thought he'd be home. Why he never asked how my day went, or how the kids were doing in school. Why he never told me how attractive he still found me, how he enjoyed my sense of humor, or how much he admired my work. Why we never sat down to chat over a cup of coffee.

I'd given up hope he would ever get up from his damned computer, kiss me tenderly on the back of my neck, and run a bath for me with lavender bubbles. I wanted him to pour a glass of wine, sit down next me, and pile bubbles on my head the way he did with the kids when they were little. After which we would fix a bite to eat, finish off the bottle, and curl up together for the night. The way it should be.

While Kate waited for me to sort this all out, I tried to imagine what it would be like to be loved by someone when you had been cast off because you were too old or too heavy. To have someone welcome you into his life when you were feeling obsolete. To go off with someone who would overlook your imperfections and embrace you in spite of them. I tried to envision what it would be like to walk away with another man, smiling and warm and loving—but I couldn't. Instead, I saw myself alone on a path in the woods. Alone on the beach at sunset. Alone in an empty church.

"I'm sorry," she said.

"No, it's okay. It's fine," I said. "At least, now I know."

Meaning, finally I knew the truth, and I understood it. A sense of relief washed over me like a passing shower on a summer day. At long last, I saw a way out. A legitimate excuse to call it quits. A compelling reason to move on after forty-two years of marriage. I wasn't surprised. I wasn't angry, or hurt, or bitter.

The truth released me.

If that surprised Kate, she didn't let on. She knew what I was thinking.

Marriage is not meant to be lived in solitude, fear, or regret. It is not meant to be an empty promise. A dead-end road. A prison. If this is what your marriage feels like, you may want to appeal your case. Jump bail. Free yourself.

Marriage should be a safe haven. A welcoming embrace. A soothing balm for everything you imagine is wrong with you, but isn't.

Your spouse should be your rock. Your anchor. A wellspring of understanding, affirmation, and consolation. If it feels like you go to bed with a stranger every night, you might be happier with a puppy. If your husband is shifting sand, the tide may already have gone out. If he is thistledown on the wind, let him go.

When you do, I hope you have a friend like Kate, because you're going to need someone who knows how to patch up a broken heart, to soak up tears, to sit still and stay calm when the tectonic shift occurs. It helps to have someone to walk in the woods with you. Somebody to watch the sun set with you and to kneel beside you in prayer.

Which is why, I believe, women gather like this, at their favorite restaurant for a bite to eat, or around the kitchen table for a cup of tea, or for a brisk walk on a well-worn trail. You can't tell by looking at them what they're up against. You can't see their broken hearts or crushed spirits, so it can be hard to pick them out of the crowd. They get out of bed in the morning like the rest of us. There is nothing strange or special about the way they dress. They get their children off to school, and tend to the house, or go to their jobs. They are right there behind us in the checkout line at the grocery store, on the treadmill next to us at the gym, and around our kitchen tables. Wherever we go, we encounter people whose pain doesn't show so we don't recognize it. If we did, we would gather all of them in. We would hear them out and lift them up.

These are not idle gatherings.

They are sacred circles that comfort and support us, connecting us across time and space. The forces that keep us connected are brute strength, manifest wisdom, and pure joy, which, when you think about it, should be impossible.

It isn't, though.

When your path in life takes an unexpected turn, it may lead you out of the woods. When the sun goes down, you get to watch the stars come out. If you can sit together quietly and patiently, applause breaks out. The moment you speak the truth, the cheering gets louder. If you accept it, the whole universe celebrates.

By the time Kate and I were ready to leave that night, the regulars had all gone home. While the kitchen crew cleaned up and the bartender mopped the floor, we started gathering up the leftover fragments of our patchwork lives. I swear, I heard applause.

We packed up the pieces that still didn't seem to fit and left the rest on the table behind us. The cheering grew louder. I smiled.

Let the celebration begin.

Forgiving Betty Tyme
by Misty Tyme

*I had to give up the fantasy that she would
tell me how sorry she was.*

My mom, Betty Tyme, had an hourglass figure, deep black hair, and large, round, crystal blue eyes. She was born with a talent few have, and beauty that she used skillfully. Her soulful singing voice was phenomenal and seeing her perform live was a magical experience.

Betty Tyme knew how to work a crowd and charm any man she had in her sights.

She was always at the center of any party. Her life resembled a juicy novel that was set in the heyday of Hollywood, with cocktails, sex, and rumors of the Mafia. My mother and the famous Elizabeth Taylor could have been sisters. With more than looks and talent in common, they both collected husbands. My mom's husband count was six, plus one live-in boyfriend. She had five children, although she didn't look like it. Marilyn

Monroe would have envied her figure—and she knew Marilyn, along with many of the other big names back then.

After her first husband (who was the true love of her life and rumored to be in the Mafia) had left her, she fell back on her incredible talent, eventually earning a record contract with Dot Records. She worked at all the big clubs in Los Angeles, Palm Springs, and Las Vegas. She named me Misty, inspired by a song.

Mom was singing at the Sahara Hotel in Las Vegas when a music director for the big nightly show found out she was pregnant and said, "If you have a girl, name her Misty," after the hit song, released in 1959.

The spotlight loved Betty Tyme, following her everywhere she went; it needed her, and she needed it. "I am the star," she would say. Not only was she a star onstage, but she needed to be the star in every aspect of her life.

If anyone or anything threatened to outshine her, it brought out my mother's dark side.

It is common for mothers and daughters to have struggles. However, my mom did not struggle—she battled. If you were not a skilled debater, it was not a good idea to tangle with her. She would detect your weakness and, in a few sentences, you'd be so terrified, you'd admit to anything. My mother had lifelong clashes with relatives, neighbors, and even random strangers.

Her passionate ability to argue made all her children's lives rough. She, and whoever she was currently married to, would get into alcohol-fueled arguments that either ended with them passing out or walking out. Betty kept her children fed and clothed, but she did not manage to shield any of us from the chaos of her choices. Children who grow up in this type of pain, as many children do, often develop a deep resentment over the childhood lived and a longing for the childhood that could have been.

One drama would pass, and then we would move on to the next adventure, or the next marriage. As a result, we would change schools and houses about every two years. All of us children always had the sense that we were in the way of her career or our next stepfather. When I was about twelve, she yelled at me, "If I had not had children, I would have been a big star."

I have a sense that she was right.

We knew we were loved, but we did not know if we were safe.

Betty Tyme made big leaps in her life. She leapt into relationships, projects, and even businesses, feet first. Most of her leaps were uninformed jumps from a cliff. All the men she picked abused her. She had been beaten, raped, and left by the men who supposedly loved her. She was always left with her children and no partner to rely on.

Was my mom, Betty Tyme evil? Did my mom want to hurt us like this? None of her children ever felt she was trying to hurt us. In fact, mom always made a big deal over birthdays or any holiday. Her ability to cook was legendary, and our table was always filled with warm, wholesome food. She had a hard-working and adventurous spirit, which all of her children inherited.

She just made seriously bad decisions.

If you had the guts and nerve to ask her version of past events, you would get a very different tale. Mom was never wrong when it came to the decisions she made. She felt she was making choices that would provide for her children. These choices included marrying men whom she did not love. One of the men she married had tried to rape her best friend. But mom was losing her house in a foreclosure and she felt she needed him, or we would have been homeless.

As I grew, so did my seething resentment toward my mother and my difficult family life.

During the first day of my senior year of high school, I moved out of my house. I worked two jobs and finished high school early. I had to get away from the vodka-driven quarrels that happened like clockwork every night. Surprisingly, my mom was excited for me. She helped me decorate and made sure my cabinets were full of food.

Years later, when I was married and had my first child, she was supportive and helpful. My mom loved babies. The trouble would begin when the babies grew into young children. If they mentioned their other grandmother, she was instantly jealous, feeling the spotlight pulled from her. If one of the kids did not notice her and tell her how pretty she was, she would exclaim that the child was a brat.

When Husband Number Six left her, after cheating with the neighbor, Betty Tyme picked herself up again and started singing. She began singing at a local club and put out a new CD. At age seventy-four, she still had a remarkable voice. She also had a new boyfriend, and they moved in together. Her grown children were thrilled. Mom was always easier to deal with when she had a romance in her life.

A few years later, the live-in boyfriend noticed some changes in her behavior. He explained that she would make plans to do something and then totally forget. When he would mention the plans, she would fly off the handle, accusing him of drinking too much. Soon, the live-in boyfriend left, because my mom's behavior had gotten more difficult than usual. The boyfriend was less abusive than my mom's six husbands, but no match for my mother's ability to disagree.

I went with my mom to her family practice physician.

The doctor skillfully distracted her by having a nurse take her away for a test. That is when he told me he was sure she had dementia. Because her musical ability had remained intact, her brain had been able to hide her disease longer than normal. But alcohol had taken a toll. Even in her late seventies, she would drink two to three screwdrivers a night, heavy on the vodka, light on the orange juice.

She had many head traumas from all the spousal abuse. Her poor brain was both pickled and bruised. My mom's downward slide came fast, changing the diagnosis to Alzheimer's Dementia. Soon, she could no longer live alone. My older siblings tried to help, but it became apparent that I was the one who would need to handle her care.

The next step was a locked memory care facility. I found a great place not far from my home. It was warm and lovely. She would have her own apartment, minus a stove, as she could no longer be trusted to cook. Call me evil or a genius, but I knew I would have to lie to get her there. I told her that I had found a senior living apartment complex that was like being on a cruise ship—with a full restaurant and eligible men. I had her interest immediately.

What I did not mention was she would no longer have her car or the option to cook. She would also have to give up her beloved dog. She thought the apartment was too small and she noticed the kitchen was without a stove. I lied again and told her that this was not her permanent apartment, as they were remodeling hers. Because of her disease, she believed me.

Soon, she did not notice the lack of a stove or that she never moved into her remodeled apartment. Her downhill slide accelerated.

She still had a whopper of a temper and would show it—until the day came when she forgot why she was mad. That is when Alzheimer's Dementia became a blessing. You have to remember why you are mad to stay mad.

Then my mother lost the memory of almost everyone in her life, including the men who hurt her and all the regrets of lost stardom. As her anger fell away, she truly was in the moment, because the moment was all she had. However, she never forgot the first love of her life, the handsome Italian she had married when she was just seventeen.

Even while caring for her, I still held onto much of my bitterness.

But I would stuff it down so I could do this job as lovingly as possible. I saw her every day. Sometimes I would be at her facility three times a day. I was in charge of all the decisions in her life. I would take her out to Sunday brunch each week and take her shopping.

My mom was still experiencing the consequences of her life decisions, even if she no longer knew why. Only a few of her grown children and grandchildren would visit. Other family members had a hard time even calling her. She was the poster child for how not to live your life.

One day near Christmas, when I was visiting her, she looked up at me and asked if I was Misty. I said yes. She took my hand and tears rolled down her face. She said that she loved me, and she did not know who she was anymore. At that moment, she was not the lady who made bad decisions that hurt her children—she was just a little old lady who needed me to hold her hand and tell her that I loved her.

Living in the moment with my mother allowed me to start working on forgiving her.

Throughout her whole life, she strived for admiration and love. She demanded it! Now I felt sorry for the woman who never could find completeness in knowing that she was perfect just as God had made her.

I had to give up the fantasy that she would tell me how sorry she was for all the drama she put my siblings and me through. She did not remember the pain, and she was no longer self-justifying her past. I realized I could still love her, even with all the mistakes she had made. My bitterness melted away.

A few months later, she became ill and her health declined rapidly. She saw the love of her life, the handsome Italian first husband, a few days before she died, although we never saw him. In a very clear voice and with determination she said, "I have to go. He has come to take me on a date."

I held her hand and told her to go.

I imagine her now in heaven on a magnificent stage, singing and dancing, while six husbands cheer her on.

The One Love That Lasts
by Tamara Knox

Radical change is sometimes necessary to find our true selves.

He came into my life after Spirit gave me the nudge to start dating again. The signs were loud and clear in dreams, coincidences, and energetic patterns of light. Now, I kissed him goodbye with an enormous love in my heart and told him we would see each other in three days.

Little did I realize the extent to which this kiss would change my life forever.

Our relationship had started about two years earlier when his deceased mother began assisting us from the "other side" to become closer. She would communicate in a whispered voice and dreams, telling me to text him messages. She showed me specific occurrences that happened in his life so we could talk about them. Our discussions lasted hours, and we developed a very strong bond.

During my hardships with illness and confusion, he was right there with me, supportive and strong. We danced endlessly with each other—body, mind, and soul. Every day was a blessing and an opportunity to feel loved. It was the best love affair: open, honest, raw, exciting, and fun.

He was my soulmate. Our relationship was sacred, offering love and comfort in a way that other relationships never could. As soulmates, we were a strong vibrational match, dimensionally linked, and able to come together in loving ways when challenges and life situations became hard.

The day I kissed him goodbye with all that love in my heart, I had no idea it would be a true goodbye.

As the plane door closed behind me, the portal for change opened, and my life after that would never be the same.

I flew to California for an author's retreat, hoping that three full days of writing would help me to get clear ideas about a book I wanted to pen. But sitting silent in a conference room with other authors, I began to feel warm, fidgety, and uncomfortable.

At the time, I wasn't sure what was being created, but knew I needed space to get some clarity. I politely excused myself from the group, explained I would be back in a short while, and left the building with no destination in mind.

As a water element, my natural gravitation is toward water, so my higher self led me to Manhattan Beach in LA, a short drive from the retreat. Once my feet hit the sand, I knew this was the right place for me and I started to feel more like myself. My perfect spot on the beach was away from the crowd.

There I sat with a little bag of gems, a merkaba in my hand, my purse, sunhat, and water bottle; not much, but the essentials for comfort. My merkaba symbol was a shape made of two intersecting tetrahedrons that spin in opposite directions, creating a three-dimensional energy field to provide protection and transport consciousness to higher dimensions.

A seagull captivated me for a moment. Then something profound happened.

"You don't need anything, just look at me," the seagull said.

Instantly, the seagull took my heart and soul into the vastness of the Universe.

We were connected in a way that was beyond limits. The vastness that became conscious in me was like no other experience I had ever known. Although my eyes had limited distance of vision, there was another part of me that was infinite and connected to infinity. I fully absorbed it.

The energies that were included in this experience were beyond belief. No words could express my feeling of *wow*, which was an awareness that kept me silent and in awe. I did not return to the retreat, nor did I continue writing that day. I sat in this sacred dimension for hours; silent, blissful, and in love. Although the seagull was long gone, our connection continued and grew stronger.

This was love at its highest, a true connection to the Divine.

I returned to the hotel where the retreat was being held and went straight to my room. Still in an expanded state, I needed to rest quietly. As the night continued, things about my life were becoming clearer. I was able to be in the present and sit with a peaceful breath while looking into the past without judgment or guilt. There was no fear, no apprehension, and no doubt as I saw my future with much more clarity and certainty.

Something in me changed, and although I wasn't sure what, time would tell. I decided it would be best to lay low and kept my retreat writing to a minimum. After saying a quiet goodbye to everyone, I boarded the plane, excited to get back to my hometown and my relationship.

Upon arriving home, everything appeared the same—but it wasn't, at least not for me. The house, kids, friends, soulmate were just the way they had been when I left. I was different. My seagull experience was still with me, and returning to my old life was not making much sense, especially the life with my soulmate.

The love was there, but I was not.

I tried to reconnect as my mind kept telling me how perfect the love was, but my heart and soul knew it wasn't the perfection I had encountered at the beach. Now, when I was with my soulmate, I felt an emptiness I had never felt before. There was an energy he could never match, and I longed for it, determined to keep it alive.

When I was without him, writing, meditating, or taking a walk, I would have the love. But when I was with him, it would disappear. This was confusing to me. I needed an explanation! Where did our love go?

How could I go from madly in love to emotionally empty over the course of a few days?

In meditation, my clear intention was to understand why the seagull had appeared and how it was connected to my soulmate and the change. Within a few days, answers came that made me sad and excited at the same time; sad, because I was guided to say goodbye to my soulmate and the relationship, but excited for something new from Divine guidance.

I had always trusted Spirt and had no concerns about being led to do that which was best for my path, family, future, and soul. I had to trust, be brave, and delicately inform my soulmate that our amazing, magical, unlike-no-other-love relationship would be ending.

This breakup was going to be hard, emotional, raw, open, and honest.

During the days since my return, he had already felt me pulling away, so he wasn't surprised when I said we needed to talk. However, he was surprised when I told him a seagull on the beach had taken me into another dimension to see multiple lifetimes and expansion, and now I was being guided through meditation and Spirit to explore self-love rather than relationship love. He was extremely confused and disheartened. He did know that there was no way to stop me on this journey or try to rewire my brain to see things differently.

He looked at me with a sad heart and said, "It's usually the things that bring people together that tear them apart."

He fell in love with me because of my spiritual practices and journey and he understood that they were now pulling us apart. We held each other for hours and cried, knowing this was goodbye. This sweet sorrow created a profound learning experience in my life and answered the questions, "Why do we have soul-relationships, and why do they suddenly end?"

The choice to be in a relationship is profoundly personal.

My soul is on its own path and timeline with love. Challenges in my soul relationship helped me grow and become a better human and more experienced lover. The love transformed, healed, inspired, created life, and brought about magic in my world. My soulmate relationship was the foundation for me to surrender enough to Spirit so that I was able to trust there was something more for my soul to experience.

As I said goodbye to my old relationship, an incredible new love came my way. It was not a physical or emotional love, but rather a spiritual love from Divine Source that continues to fuel me every day. I believe my new love is the sacred energy that inhabits all of creation, the one love, the one source.

For my own journey, I realized that I could not focus on both a soulmate relationship and a Divine-centered relationship. Divine energies were guiding me to commit to other areas in my life, which didn't leave energy or create a strong vibration for my soulmate.

My Divine message was to focus on family, health, friendships, and career in new ways.

As I committed to meditation, rest, and trusting Source, everything fell into alignment. As my immune system got stronger, I was able to spend more quality time with my children, my writing, and other projects that appeared in my life. In addition, my relationship with Spirit got stronger. I was happy and began to experience again the spiritual expansion felt that day on the beach.

It was exactly what my soul needed; to see love in a whole new way, a more conscious, gentler side of the equation.

Radical change is sometimes necessary to find our true selves.

When in a relationship with myself, love becomes the essence of the Universe. My gift of merging with the seagull was seeing the pieces of myself I had forgotten or didn't know. That connection allowed me to understand love in a new way, to flatter myself, and to begin a life with new ideas and a new reference point. I now know the higher essence available to me when I slow down and trust my feelings and intuition.

My self-love defines the power of the Divine. It is the highest love and holds the highest essence. To be able to know myself with complete intimacy opens doors for higher blessings, beauty, the ability to create, true happiness, and self-discovery. Self-love is the best mystery, with no goodbyes.

He Had Me at Mary Oliver
by Laura Staley

I now know what a "good fit" relationship feels,
smells, looks, tastes, and sounds like.

With encouragement from a friend, I chose to courageously leap into the world of online dating.

Signing up on a site, a Sherpa guide would have been helpful, as I had no idea what I was doing. In response to "Who are you looking for?" I wrote, "Someone who will make me laugh."

Pondering the question, "What is your username?" my love of the poetry of Mary Oliver came to mind. My favorite poem was "Wild Geese." I figured the dude out in internet land would know that "MO" are the initials for Mary Oliver, that he would be familiar with her beautiful poetry, so I created my username: WildGeeseMO11.

After initially freaking out over the "blow up" of email messages that arrived, I got brave and opened one. Thinking to myself, this guy was born in 1969, I clicked PassionPlay69. He shared about liking the Buckeyes, dark chocolate, and walking in the woods. He let me know he was a social drinker and asked if I liked s'mores.

"I like the Buckeyes, chocolate, and walking in the woods. I don't drink but do have plenty of friends who enjoy a glass of wine. No problem with the social drinking. I'm gluten-free so can't do the graham crackers, but do like toasted marshmallows and chocolate. Haven't had a s'more in years," I replied.

That morning on my run, I kept wondering about "PassionPlay69" and then the translation hit me. OMG!! I did the Eeew dance, met with one of my closest women friends later that day, and told her everything.

"You are not going walking in the woods with this guy. No! You never put "wild" in anything on the internet with dudes and dating! And we must look up *s'mores* in Urban Dictionary! You must shut down your profile on that site! Today!"

"What's Urban Dictionary?" I quietly asked as I had no clue.

"A dictionary for slang used on the internet. Oh, here's what s'mores means! OMG!"

Immediately, I closed my account.

I chose to go the old-fashioned route to meet a kind, self-aware man in person. The self-aware part did not immediately happen. Turns out, I was fortunate to learn from another all-too-familiar experience.

While networking for business, I met a man, and we began dating. Very quickly, the dynamic of interaction felt familiar in that "not a good fit" way. The deep-seated unworthiness, the shame-fear that first heated up inside my chest and then burned red on my cheeks emerged regularly. I felt ashamed of my difficult past, my failed marriage, and the many challenges I had recently navigated, yet wasn't willing to hide when the topics organically came up. I knew enough not to pretend about my life. When this gentleman would say unkind things about me in front of other people as a joke, I witnessed the sensations in my body but remained silent. His insecurities expressed as arrogance did an interesting dance with my unworthiness, feelings of smallness, and my deep yearning to be loved and accepted.

My Inner Fly on the Wall

Because I had been meditating daily for more than a year, I noticed these patterns from my Inner Fly on the Wall, that part of me that quietly watched me do me and this man do and be himself. During this time, my old, unhealthy pattern of words and deeds had ended. Not once did I attempt to fix, correct, change, ridicule, manipulate, cajole, shame, or lash out at him. I silently observed his ways of interacting with me. A newfound freedom allowed me to express my care and to be creative, playful, and sexy.

In my mind, I threw yellow flags when he spoke words that stung or deflected a kindness offered. These internal flags accumulated over a few months and quickly taught me that we did not share similar values, interests, or languages of love. When he'd drop me off after a date, I'd weep with a mixture of unworthy feelings, a yearning to be with him, and an overwhelming sense of rejection, as well as a flood of gratitude that I had experienced some companionship to break up my loneliness and touch deprivation.

The final straw came after creating a collage gift for him on his birthday. The collage contained images of many things he loved, including his childhood hometown, the car he loved to drive, the lake he loved visiting with his family, and activities he enjoyed. When I presented it to him at a restaurant dinner party with his friends, he looked at it laughed. "You have too much time on your hands."

Once again, the shame-fear stirred deep inside me. The stronger, healthier part of me knew that we simply were not a good fit. The witness part of me noticed his deflection. I said nothing. As he turned away to interact with his best friend, one of his other friends approached me and said, "That was a really kind and thoughtful gift you created."

"Thank you for appreciating it," I replied.

His friend's ability to verbally appreciate my gift also seemed to amplify our not-good-fit situation. Sitting at dinner, listening to his friends discuss politics, I quietly ate. It was time to end our dating experience and to tackle the work inside of me to discover my value.

A few days later, I broke my silence with him and shared my experiences as honestly as possible, including many of the interactions that had felt hurtful, while acknowledging that I had much inner work to do. I still desired a healthy, vibrant, love relationship—but what we had wasn't it.

While I loved myself, I still struggled to value myself.

In the aftermath of our break-up, I grieved while continuing to passionately believe I could experience a quality love relationship. I confronted the possibility of remaining single for the remainder of my life, including not ever making love with a man again. Removing the framed art piece in my bedroom of a single woman with her back to me, I created and hung a collage of images of couples laughing, holding hands, and kissing in natural settings. I continued exercising, meditating, eating healthy food, and spending time with friends.

Journaling every single day for twenty-one days about what I wanted to experience in a love relationship allowed me to weep, as all my lifelong dreams poured out into words. "Self-aware" showed up all over the pages.

On Day 22, I burned all of that ink and paper on a cold, starry February night, out on my patio, a few days after Valentine's Day.

One year and seven months after closing down the internet dating site, and two months after burning the journal on my patio, I attended a Singles Mingle Meet-up at a restaurant where eight men and four women gathered.

Having done a great deal of business networking, I chose to view this experience in a similar light. Introducing myself to two gentlemen and a lady, I listened as they shared about travel, art museums, and their favorite national parks. I shared about being an author, showed them my book, and let them know how important nature, being outside, and experiencing beautiful artwork was to me. I gave the two men my business card and got ready to leave, as I had another commitment. One gentleman literally twinkled at me when he smiled. Later that evening, he sent an email asking to meet for coffee.

I replied, "Yes, but I don't usually drink coffee."

He responded, "That's okay. I don't drink coffee."

This became one small "in common" of a thousand.

We met and hit it off quite beautifully. I really enjoyed his company and our conversation. We walked outside at parks and through neighborhoods after getting a beverage. On our third date, while sitting across from each other in a Panera, an unusual lull in the conversation prompted me to ask him, "Do you enjoy reading?"

"Well, yes. Lately I've been reading the poetry of Mary Oliver before I go to sleep at night."

"Yaaaaaaah!" I screamed with delight while waving my arms in the air.

My entire internet debacle story became the new conversation. He laughed then asked how he could be of service. When my truth about wanting to be in a love relationship was shared, he said he wasn't looking.

"We could be friends, and I could date a bunch of men."

The playful interacting and laughing continued as he walked me to my minivan. When he asked to purchase my book, I handed him a copy. He then said, "You know, I'm open to love," and gently kissed me before we parted ways.

Almost a year after meeting, we relocated to Black Mountain, North Carolina.

We recently celebrated three years of our unexpected, ease-filled, tender, passionate, love-centered, emotionally healthy intimate relationship that continues to expand my heart. I learned to soften, uncoil, and receive all the ways he shows his love. What a thrill each time he receives my gratitude and creative expressions of all five languages of love and more.

I live an unrecognizable life, a bonus round of being alive here in the beauty of the mountains and in the intersection of our love for each other. I now know how a "good fit" relationship feels, smells, looks, tastes, and sounds. He often describes being with me like patiently sitting on a bench while listening with curiosity and delight as I get on a rollercoaster ride full of emotions inside a heart story that becomes an airplane ride that seems like it might never land. But then when it does, he discovers we have been in each other's arms all along, smiling, and deeply accepting each other on this delicious adventure.

A Healthy Love Story
by Kristi Tornabene

Looks are fleeting and only skin deep.

The attraction was instant as my eyes followed the professor to the front of the classroom. *What a body!* I thought as he passed my desk. *And cute butt. But he's old enough to be my father.* My uncensored thoughts made me blush and glance around the room to see if anyone was watching me watch him. They weren't. They were all watching him.

Damn, I can't believe I'm reacting like this to a professor. But the truth is, my respect for well-toned bodies ran deep because as an avid "work-out-girl" I knew time and energy went into staying in shape.

He turned and, with a perfect smile, greeted the class I had not wanted to take. "Good morning. My name is Professor Tom Tornabene, and you are in microbiology."

Oh, yeah—nothing like a little eye candy to turn a dreaded hour into a time of anticipation. The class I had resisted taking because it would overload my semester schedule now had flipped from a dreaded class to a favorite one. My day brightened.

I was young, in perfect shape and health. Life was my cake, and I could eat as much of it as I wanted without suffering physical or emotional consequences—or so I thought. This microbiology class would change my life on many levels.

Life changed everything, including my perfect body.

The attraction between us must have been mutual because, to my surprise, a month later, Professor Tornabene made the first move. "If you're on your way to class," he said, pulling up beside me in his car, "hop in, and I'll take you. I'm going in the same direction."

The temptation to slide next to him was so strong it was tangible.

"No, thanks. I have another stop to make first. See you in class."

The words were almost painful as they left my mouth. A girlfriend had told me he was married, so there was no chance of me accepting a ride from him or anything else for that matter. There would be no "us." A married man was hands-off, a no-no, to me.

But time was on my side. The situation changed. It wasn't long after the class ended that my friend said, "Did you hear the news? Professor Tornabene is getting a divorce. But he has also sworn off women."

My heart jumped.

The words were like waving a red cape in front of a bull.

"We'll see about that!" I said. And the love-chase was on.

Our first social event was at a graduation party for someone who had received their master's degree under Tom's tutelage. We didn't spend much time talking to each other that day; there were too many people in the room. I could feel his ex-wife eyeing me for some unknown reason. Perhaps the pheromones were gaining ground.

The second date was spent in conversation, learning more about each other. "I won a wrestling scholarship to Notre Dame," he said casually.

He probably thought the expression on my face was admiration for his intelligence. It was more adoration for his buff body.

Would our age difference become our glue or our undoing?

Tom was practically the same age as my father. And then there was the issue of his three kids. I wanted three children, anyway, so how bad could an instant family be, right?

The next hurdle was my family. My mother was not happy.

"It's not just his age that is my issue," she said at dinner. "Or his three kids from another woman that, by marriage, will become my grand-children. It's both of them together!"

Dad kept his thoughts to himself.

But, in the end, Tom knew how to win over my mom's heart. He built a deck onto the house for her and quickly gained her approval. I was ready for the wedding bells.

Two years passed. Tom did not propose. Although our relationship was not moving forward, time was not standing still. My biological clock was ticking. Perhaps a bit of jealousy and an ultimatum was needed to move us forward.

"You better ask me to marry you, or I will end this relationship and go back to the guy in Arkansas I dated before you," I told him.

It worked. We got married. We were a beautiful couple.

Age can be a cruel master to the body.

The bells of bliss morphed into a bone of contention that built up between us: my weight gain. The assumption that I could maintain my previously athletic body went out the window with the birth of three children, followed by menopause.

His verbal badgering about my diet and weight bordered on abuse. As much as I wanted to be able to eat whatever I wanted, as I once could—and as he still did—my female body reacted differently to the ravages of time.

My love of science, along with my experience as a medical technologist, gave me an advantage over most people trying to control their weight. This became my focus and, as an adult woman, lessons from my college microbiology class came into play.

I discovered that being thin didn't necessarily mean being healthy. One evening, while seeing food and dieting commercials on TV, it occurred to me my diet, weight, health, and wellness issues were experienced by women worldwide, especially as they aged. This was not just my concern or battle. It was the focus of many high-priced commercials that had to do with body and emotional images. Weight and emotions went together.

But the commercials made everything look so easy, as thin, happy people full of self-confidence ran and danced across the screen. Their confidence felt unfair to someone with low self-esteem. So unfair!

So, I decided to ask God to help me let go of what had become an "I'm not good enough" mentality, which was exacerbated by my husband's dissatisfaction with my weight.

I was not going to take pills or supplemental diet foods.

The myriad of health and wellness information available both in books and online kept me digging deeper to find the eating plan that would work best for me. Much of my success was due to trial and error. Little did I know at the time that the pages of information gathered, and documentation of my personal experimentation, would become the basis for my book, *Keys 2 Basic Health.*

Fortunately, I did not have to make all these life-changes alone. My friend Sallie from Medical Technology School became the answer to my prayers. Together, we changed our eating, diet, and life habits. It was easier when we supported each other. Sallie's wellness story was added to my book because it was part of the healing of our minds and bodies.

Although my journey to wellness had started because of Tom's badgering, it really got underway when my digestive tract began begging for mercy with every chocolate bar eaten. Trips to the bathroom were painful and embarrassing. I was responsible for clogging the toilet at work!

My carefree days of eating everything and anything indeed were over.

It was time to create healthy digestion to relieve pain, create more energy, clear out my brain fog, and avoid repeating my family history of illnesses that could potentially plague me in old age.

Inflammation was one of the causes of my parent's ailments. Changing how and what I ate could help me avoid the same fate. The scientist in me came alive and dug into the causes and cures I was experiencing as I was aging.

Although Tom's part in my quest for wellness was mostly negative, his comments about my weight did motivate me to make changes. And his training helped answer questions like, "What's best for my body?

How much does genetics control me?" We discussed vitamin absorption, the ins and outs of amino acids, and supplementation. His advanced education in microbiology brought clarity to some of the information eventually used to make the choices that led me closer to good health.

It was easy to discuss the science of health with my husband, but he had no desire to take part in my plan to get healthy. That was entirely up to me.

One of the biggest challenges to our marriage was meals. Despite his knowledge of the science of healthy food, processed and fast foods were his favorites. And, to my extreme annoyance, he did not have my diet-related body pains or weight gains—or at least he wouldn't admit it. His diet was my body's kiss-of-death.

Was the answer to maintaining my healthy weight cooking two different meals, one for him and one for me? There had to be a better way for a healthy life and marriage.

The most significant change in my life was realizing that I am good enough. My husband's badgering helped me fulfill my dream of becoming an author with a more energetic, healthier body.

My love of science overflowed onto the pages of my life.

Although we were initially attracted to each other's physique, it was our mutual love of science that brought us together, helped us through the difficult times of growing older together, and kept the conversation going throughout the years. Looks are fleeting and only skin deep, and love is in the eye of the beholder, but my health is a blessing that must be pursued every day of my life.

Final Thoughts

Love is the ultimate happiness. Who wants to live in a world without love? Although it comes in many forms, including self-love, true love is blind and unconditional because it is a state of being that defies physical limitations.[1]

A parent's love for a child, as portrayed in the story *My Child Was Still My Child* by Lorilyn Rizzo Bridges, exemplifies a mother's undying and nonjudgmental love. And parents' emotional connections to each other affect their children's future[2], as seen in the stories. The authors wrote about the importance of embracing acceptance and forgiveness to move through relationship pain and into the joy of life. This thread of wisdom weaves throughout this section and in other parts of the book.

As many of the stories pointed out, actions speak louder than words. The language of love is real, universal, and not limited to words. The stories validate data published in developmental psychology that states love is a learned, emotional reaction. Current research has been brought to life and validated in these stories. One cannot teach what is not understood. Love is a learned language that begins in the family. To give love, you must possess love.

Self-love, shared in Tamora Knox's story, can be just as illusive, challenging, and vital as the love shared between people. Falling in love with ourselves can require as much work and attention as a new relationship.

Love never dies. Relationships built on love can last lifetimes, as seen in the story *Love Between Lives* by Rev. Ariel Patricia. Love is a powerful emotional and psychological force that makes our world go 'round—or can bring it to a screeching halt. Lasting love is a gift.

And, no matter what kind of love it is, love matters. The stories in this section shared how love is both a magical mystery and deliberate mastery. Despite all its poetic contemplation, psycho-scientific dissection, and anthropological exploration, love is what life is all about. How we handle love can be one of the things that has a direct effect on our health, as described in the next section, *Health and Well-being: I'll Stand by You*.

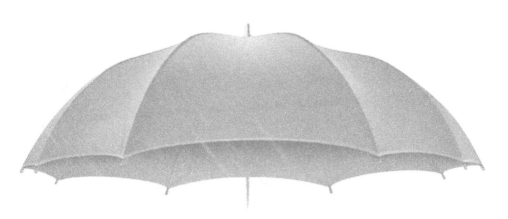

PART 2

HEALTH AND WELL-BEING
I'll Stand by You

My small self thinks
"I have lessons to learn."
My sacred self knows
"I have wisdom to gain."

Breathe! Just Breathe

by Kathleen O'Keefe-Kanavos

A good joke and a cat's purr turned a
crappy day into a happy future.

reathe! I tell myself as the kitchen begins to spin. My ears ring. My hands grip the countertop as another panic attack washes over my body and tightens its invisible stranglehold on my throat. The pounding of my heart, mixed with the clanging in my ears, is almost deafening. My desperate gasping for breath attracts the attention of both Baby Cakes—my twenty-six pound, eighteen-year-old Siamese cat crouching at my feet—and my husband, who sits in the adjoining TV room.

"Are you okay?" he shouts and turns in his recliner to listen for signs of life.

"Yeah, I was stifling a sneeze," I reassure him.

Baby Cakes pats my leg and waits to be picked up and hugged. Right now, I don't want to get any more attentive hugs, or to give any. I just want to be able to take a deep breath and not feel like someone has just jumped out from behind the door and screamed, "BOO!"

Since the frightening outcome of my exploratory surgery three days earlier, I have been unconsciously holding my breath. I'm not even aware of it until dizziness begins to overtake my body and mind. Only then, on the verge of fainting, is there temporary relief from my horrific reality. *I might die! My mother died of cancer! Breathe!*

Another big gulp of air saves me from fainting. The tissue full of tears glides over an already-spotless countertop for the fourth or fifth time. The exact number escapes me, as does the memory of picking up the tissue. My body movements are on autopilot and my mind is too unfocused to count. I feel like I am standing outside my body, watching myself go through the motions of life.

My panic attack symptoms are the same ones experienced while scuba diving in the open ocean with sharks. But the sharks were not this scary. I mastered my attacks then by focusing on something funny. Anything funny! My underwater laughter was a sound to behold. It freaked the sharks out and worked to steady my breathing, even with a scuba regulator in my mouth and a dive mask on my face. So maybe it can work now, while diving into an ocean of medical crisis and facing a different type of deadly predator—breast cancer.

The panic attacks began after my surgeon, Dr. Wagner, phoned to let us know that the preliminary pathology report on a suspicious area removed from my left breast a few days ago was indeed cancerous. He expressed surprise at the findings; the three mammograms he had ordered and physical exams he had performed had missed the area—all three times.

Fortunately, my recurrent precognitive dreams had spurred me to self-advocate for exploratory surgery. What my doctor had expected to be a non-malignant fibrosis turned out to be a cancerous tumor.

The medical pathology report validated my dream. What a nightmare.

"The preliminary pathology report states the tumor appears to be less than two centimeters, which is the beginning of stage one," he reassures me when my silence screams my fear. "I don't expect anything to be in the lymph nodes during your next procedure, which will also check for clear margins around the cancerous area, to be sure all the malignant cells were removed. A surgical oncologist will perform that procedure," he said.

I remember requesting an oncologist be present during my exploratory surgery. My request was denied because, "You are too young for breast cancer, and it does not run in your family." If my request had been accepted, all the surgery could have been done at that time, perhaps making this additional surgery unnecessary. Listening on the line, I wonder if my doctor considered it as well.

BREATHE!

"Ductal carcinoma-in-situ breast cancer is very treatable," my doctor repeats. "The final pathology report after the second surgery will tell us more."

I push the phone closer to my ear because his voice seems to be fading. Is this the result of hysterical deafness—which is something like hysterical blindness?

What's worse than being diagnosed with a life-threatening illness? Waiting for the final pathology report to find out just how sick you really are. *Breathe! Just breathe.*

Despite the effort to reassure me, I have been struggling to catch my breath ever since he called.

After hanging up, I am left with the nagging question, "*Why me?*"

Was my diet poor? Did I roll in bug spray when I was a baby? What the heck did I do wrong to deserve this?

Finding a quiet spot in my library, I meditate on the question. The answer is quite impressive.

"*Why not! You are part of Team Earth, where the ultimate goal is to experience as much life as possible until it is time for you to die and return to where you were before you were born. It is part of your destiny and earthbound experience.*"

The rule for the Game of Life seemed so simple before my cancer diagnosis; live. Now the rules seem to have changed, and I don't want to play anymore. Rather than fight this disease, I want to run away and hide, take my bat and ball and go home. Or, I could jump into my car and bolt.

Yeah, but how would that help? an inner voice asks. *It's not like running away from an unbearable relationship or a miserable job.*

So true! The problem is in the physical part of me, from which there is no escape. No matter where I go, there I'll be … with "it"… cancer. There's only one place where it cannot follow.

Suicide would be a true escape, because I'd leave my body and *crisis* behind, and never have to deal with the fear of cancer, anxiety attacks, or treatment anymore.

There's my dark, dangerous thought again.

"Get hold of yourself, Kat. Do you really want to leave? You can, but what a waste. This crisis may be challenging, but that's life. Life is hard! And remember, difficulty, pain, or bad luck is relative and a matter of perception. So what's it gonna be? Fight or flight? Live or die? We all have to be together in this decision, because if we don't hang together, we'll hang together," my inner voice says.

The thought of hanging myself scares me. What if I don't do it right? What would I hang from? There are no rafters or beams in the house, and the dining room chandelier would never hold my weight. I'd bring down the house. Imaginary headlines in the newspaper flash across my mind, "Woman Tries to Hang Self from Chandelier, Kills Cat in Fall." How embarrassing would *that* be to read from a hospital bed?

However, there are enough pills in the medicine cabinet to kill an elephant, many of them left over from Mom's fight with cancer. Still unwilling to part with anything of hers, my bathroom contains medicine bottles with her name on them, reassurance that life with her was not a dream. In my closet, high on a shelf, sits a large, plastic Ziploc bag filled with her favorite clothes. Mom's perfume and natural smells still cling to them.

Whenever feelings of grief become overwhelming, I open the bag and breathe in — a "hit of Mama." Memories triggered by her life's perfume flood my mind and lift my heavy heart. Maybe a big hit of mama now would help me. *It would be so wonderful to see her again.*

I could make that happen by mixing her pills with my favorite vodka, pull mom's plastic bag over my head, and let her smell soothe me to sleep until I reawaken with someone who experienced what I'm going through and will understand my pain — Mom.

There is one problem with that plan, says a voice from the recesses of my mind. It is one of my inner selves, a fighting Irish who never gives up. She ruins my plastic bag plan by pointing out an important fact I'd failed to consider.

"If you kill yourself, Mom will be waiting for us when we get there and kick our butts around Heaven like a football. She fought to the very end! And, Mom does not like quitters."

Hmmm … She's right. Good point.

Let's go with Plan A: We'll stay and fight with all our inner and outer resources! This cancer crisis will not become a cruel, manipulating Svengali. We'll file the flight plan of pills, booze, bags, and hangings under Plan Y or Z.

Me, myself, and I have a new game plan now. My emotions shift from fight or flight, to fight and live! Although I feel better, it seems something important is still missing.

When I return to the kitchen, my fears follow. *"Breathe, deep breaths, Kat, deep breaths,"* the voice in my head yells. I can't believe this is still happening to me! I thought we had a plan and everything was going to be okay now. What is wrong with me? What is missing?

No matter how much air I breathe in, it isn't enough. Frustrated and frightened, I claw at my throat. If some funny memory would just pop into my head, I might be able to blow out the breath filling up all the space in my lungs and inhale to stop this damn attack. The Heimlich Maneuver used to save chokers might help—but a good joke could work, too. My mind searches for jokes used during my dives, but I'm too dizzy to focus.

"Peter, tell me a good joke."

"What? Right now? Why?" he answers, turning down the TV.

"Because I need a good laugh right now."

Silence is followed by, "Okay. What sits at the bottom of the sea and twitches?"

He waits for an answer, and when none comes, says, "Give up? A nervous wreck."

I snort in response. Yeah, how fitting on so many levels.

"Here's another one. How do you make a tissue dance? Put a little boogie in it." I look down at the crumpled tissue in my hand and laugh. When my laughing stops, my breathing returns to normal.

"How's that?" Peter calls into the kitchen. "Want some more?"

"No. No thanks. That was perfect."

"You sure? I have a great 'Knock, knock'..."

"Nope, I'm good now. Thanks."

The jokes make me realize the need to embrace the funny side of life, to keep me inhaling and exhaling. Laughter has filled me with the breath of life. It is up to me to make a conscious effort to control my thoughts and shift my focus from fear to fun, from crappy to happy.

My mental babble, coupled with the attacks and the after-effects of the anesthesia, is exhausting. I need a nap.

The closet in the bedroom beckons me. Despite my limited range of motion from stitches, the plastic bag containing a white blouse, a pair of socks, a bra, and blue shorts, easily slides from the shelf. The Ziploc has not been used in a while, but the corner opens easily. I stick in my nose to keep any precious fragrances from escaping and take a deep breath. My lungs burn from the extreme stretching.

Suddenly, I'm in the kitchen of my old home, hugging my mother and laughing about the burned chestnuts in the oven for our turkey stuffing. For one sweet moment in time, everything is alright again. I sigh. This is what had been missing—a moment in the memory of love, to forget to be frightened.

I replace the magic bag of mom-memories on the shelf … until next time.

The pain from my breast causes me to grimace as I lower myself onto the mattress. Baby Cakes climbs up behind me to *spoon* his body against me. Then he gently rests his enormous head on mine, wraps his paws around my neck, and purrs so loud it drowns out any negative thoughts that might try to creep back in. Ahhh. The effect is soothing beyond words. My body relaxes under the weight of his love.

"I could never leave you, Baby-cakes," I whisper. "We've bagged Mom. Now we need to bottle you and your purr. We'd make a mint off that purr." His paws tighten into a hug.

During the nap, I meditate on returning my body to perfection while in my ear Baby's purr echoes, "Purrfect, purrfect."

It becomes a mantra. My breath automatically times itself to his rhythmic purring as sleep blankets me. My breathing returns to normal.

A husband's joke, the smell of loving memories, a cat's purr, and a furry hug around the neck transformed my day from crappy to happy. Purrfect!

Ready to Make That Call
by Diane Vich

My soul was ready to face those demons
without triggering my downfall.

ance. Let go and just dance." I sing to myself, eyes closed while cranking up the volume. "Get lost in the rhythm." The pressures of my job as a registered nurse dealing with Covid-19 patients melts away as the music washes over my body and soul. It is my kundalini energy ritual, done before every stressful phone call to an anxious parent.

They are waiting for their child's Covid-19 test results.

As an RN, it is my responsibility to call families with the test results and tell them if their child is healthy or infected with Covid-19. When a child is healthy, dancing before the call is unnecessary. My joy at sharing good news with parents is enough to carry me through the conversation.

But the call I am about to make is a difficult one. I close my eyes again and exercise my voice in song. Music flows through my body as it sways to the beat. I smile at myself in the mirror, seeing the silly shift in my vibrations, facial expressions, and emotions. The music surrounds me as I wait for the song to end. My energetic vocal release takes my stress away and completes the shift.

I use music and dance to reconnect to my kundalini energy and empower my voice.

My own health crisis began during a highly stressful time of life. Quickly realizing prescriptions, surgeries, and conventional medicine would not be my solution, I left my knowledge and expertise in traditional nursing behind and began a journey forward into the realm of alternative healing.

I knew my illness had an underlying cause. My goal was to find it. Like other people I have heard or read about, I also possessed unique gifts that remained unacknowledged until close friends and colleagues opened my eyes to them.

My health issue had two roots: one was physical, while the other was emotional. Plagued by issues in my tissues and debilitating pain, I worked hard to find the nutrients, stress relief, exercise, and meditation to get me on track.

A variety of strategies combined to make a quick, stress-fighting routine that included hypnosis meditations, affirmations, stretching, deep breathing, singing, vocalization, and dancing. By deeply connecting with my body and following its natural flow through movements, tension, and pain, emotions are released from my tissues.

I'd never imagined the amazing, divine feminine power this unique experience creates.

My final two years of self-discovery involved a kundalini awakening, emotional enlightenment, and spiritual journey. It was this final trinity-piece that helped me realize how trauma and abuse in childhood impact adult life in exponential ways. The unique process helped align my dreams and reality to fulfill my passions without suffering through the symptoms.

This part of my spiritual trip involved working on feelings and emotions by tapping into a history I had blocked so long ago. It was the hardest part of my journey. It was easier to heal my physical pain than the emotional trauma. Getting my inner voice and intuition back took an enormous amount of effort after suppressing it for so long. The beautiful thing I learned is that the process doesn't have to be too traumatic or confusing, with the right support and resources.

My hardest success was overcoming my childhood abuse and trauma. This is a secret I share with only a privileged few. It took an interesting journey into my emotional abyss to finally understand that the lies in my subconscious mind were holding me back in life. Self-limiting beliefs that kept me stuck were slowly unraveling and diminishing. A few of those beliefs impacted my self-worth, self-esteem, confidence, and sense of safety.

I forgave and let go of the past.

I forgave those who had hurt me in my childhood by going through an intense mourning and forgiveness ritual at a spiritual retreat. As a song played, I sat in the darkness, looking into the left eye of a stranger. In that moment, connected to a stranger through her eye, I felt her pain and forgave the past. Realizing that those who hurt me didn't know any better was the birth of a deep sense of forgiveness toward them and myself. They had already hurt themselves severely with physical illness and emotional pain.

I chose to free myself of those negative emotions and self-limiting beliefs. I remember feeling free, light, and relaxed. Four days of deep inner work, forgiveness, and reflection ignited my soul and released the roots of my trauma. A deep sense of peace washed over me.

Tackling trauma is like peeling a raw onion. One layer leads to the next, but in the end, the tearful job is finally done—until you work on the next one. Little did I know that, after I finally forgave those who had hurt me, life was going to place those individuals in my path again. And this time, I was the one who supported them and their family through a tough journey that took several months to resolve.

Thankfully, my soul was ready to face those demons without triggering my downfall. My forgiveness and evolution helped me selflessly support them in their time of great need. I passed my tests. The battle is never completely over. Obstacles/onions still appear all the time.

One of the gifts I miss now that I am working from home are the triplets.

The most fundamental part of my healing process was creating a self-loving routine through awareness and action to release emotions, pain, and stress. It made me grateful for all the inspiration the world sends my way. I laugh every day when continuously blessed by nature with beautiful animals, insects, and experiences.

A gorgeous group of ducklings born months before Covid-19 always managed to find me at various locations during my outdoor breaks at the hospital. One day, while standing with my eyes closed at the edge of the water, sending a blessing to a friend, I suddenly felt movement at my feet. Three ducklings—the triplets—were rubbing against my shoes. It is truly a miraculous experience to connect deeply with nature and reap the benefits.

My transformation empowered my gifts in traditional nursing and spiritual growth. As a nurse, I use my talents daily to support myself and patients through illness and disease.

Ahh, good, I think as I finish swaying, singing, smiling, and moving.

Now, I am ready to make *that call.*

"Hello? This is Nurse Diane Vich calling for your daughter... Oh, I see … She's better, but your wife is hospitalized. … Then, I will make this call brief. I am calling with your other child's Covid-19 test results. Your daughter tested positive. How is she doing? I can hardly hear you, Sir. Are you feeling okay? Could you please speak up? Oh… you have it too and can hardly breathe."

He continues coughing and hands the phone to his eldest child to speak with me.

"Hello, this is Nurse Diane from the hospital. I was calling to check on you and your family. Your dad mentioned your mom was sick? Oh, I see, both of your parents are sick, but mom was having shortness of breath. Is she at the hospital now with your sister? Are you able to call her and advise her of the test results to help protect the staff caring for her? Sure, I understand. Give me her name, and I will notify them for you …. Yes, go ahead and help your dad. If he is having shortness of breath, he should go to the hospital, too. Have you ever used telemedicine?... Great, so if your dad needs to see a doctor, use that—but if he gets worse, he will need to come to the hospital, too ... Okay, great, stay safe and indoors. Make sure that everyone is following the quarantine and staying away from others. Feel free to call me if you have further questions or concerns."

That which I used to heal myself, I now share with others.

When life is too difficult for words, I sing to empower my voice and dance to strengthen my soul. I move beyond the crappy things that happen in life, into a place of joy, and my reward is experiencing wellness wrapped in spiritual happiness.

Power Through Surrender
by Ken Walls

I let God handle the results.

"Hey, man! I put in my two-week notice! I'll be ready to start in a couple of weeks."

Dave had just sat down next to me at the bar. I looked at him like he was from another planet and asked, "What in the world are you talking about, dude?"

"I'm ready to start working for you as your head technician!"

Immediately my brain went into overdrive. "Wait! What?"

"We discussed this the other night. You offered me the position with your company." He was starting to look like his dog had just died. There was an awkward moment of silence.

"Bro, I am downsizing my company. Things are not good right now. I'm not hiring and have no idea where you got that idea!" I tried my best to sound like the stern CEO that I was, attempting to make him think he was crazy and misinformed. Boy, did those tables get flipped on me.

Dave looked me right in the eye and said, "You don't remember our conversation the other night, do you?" Without skipping a beat, he went on. "Ya know, I'm not surprised that you don't remember. Everyone around here knows you're nothing but a drunk! Why don't you go to an AA meeting or something? Get some help!"

Then he stood up and walked out of the bar.

My seventh draft beer of the night had left me not even slightly buzzed.

My alcohol tolerance had become completely unpredictable. Sometimes, drinking a couple of beers could send me into a blackout. Other times, I could drink all night and barely get a buzz.

At this moment, I was stone cold sober and flabbergasted. Quickly, I scanned the bar to see how many people were looking at me. This dude just finished calling me a worthless drunk in front of the entire bar. My ego was badly bruised!

But then the strangest feeling swept over me. It felt as if time just stood still, like in one of those movie scenes where everyone and everything froze, and I could just walk around all of these frozen people. The sensation freaked me out.

About halfway through my eighth beer, I paid my tab, walked out of the place, and hurried back to my hotel room.

Yes...hotel. My ex had thrown me out after an incident. Apparently, I showed up at her best friend's house with a twelve-pack of beer and "other" things in mind. Another thing I did not remember happening.

My life was in a tailspin.

Everything was out of control. Every single friendship and my relationship with my family had been lost. Everyone knew I was a drunk—except me. At thirty-four years old, my life had no meaning and no purpose for being on this planet. I was at the end of my rope, not wanting to live or die. I was lost.

Back at the hotel that night, a guy I partied with once in a while called me. He knew I was in a hotel and separated from my ex.

"Dude! I have a couple of chicks with me ... let's go to the bar and party!"

"No, dude. I'm done. Sorry," I replied.

I switched off my cell phone and lay down on the hotel room bed, closed my eyes, and said out loud, "God, please help me. I cannot do this and don't know how to make it stop. If you're real, then please help me now!"

Something felt different.

The next morning, something felt different. I can't explain exactly how. Somehow, my desire to drink had been lifted. Still scared, for the first time in my life, I felt a little bit of hope. A very little bit of hope.

I decided to go to a Twelve-Step meeting that night. There was one about five minutes away, yet I couldn't take the chance of being "seen" walking into a church for an AA meeting! So, I drove to a meeting about forty miles out of town. Walking in about five minutes before it started, I sat right next to a familiar face. It was a doctor that I knew, and he recognized me! I was like ... *Crap. I can't believe I freaking know someone here!*

"Dude, what are you doing here?"

"I've been waiting for you!" he said.

At the meeting, everyone was asked to share their thoughts. I waited until I was the very last person to speak and introduced myself.

"Hi, I'm Ken, and I am an alcoholic."

"Hi, Ken!" everyone answered.

"Wow! That is the first time I've ever said that I am an alcoholic and truly believed it!" I replied.

In my mind, I had this huge speech planned to enlighten everyone in that room, but apparently, God had a different plan. Just as I was beginning to pontificate, a bat flew down from the rafters of the church and started circling the room. It swooped past me a couple of times. I swear, I might have screamed like a terrified little girl! Suddenly, I wanted out of that room, and said, "You know what? I'll just pass!"

Then the bat flew back up to its perch. We all stood in a circle, holding hands to say The Lord's Prayer. It was like God was saying, "Dude ... surrender and shut up! Let Me do My thing in your life!"

I had a stern talking-to with God.

On the drive back to my hotel, I made sure He knew I did not appreciate him using a bat to shut me up. I am not a fan of those little flying mice, which He must have already known. But I also felt just a little more hope that night, and thanked God for helping me stay sober for one day.

That night, I realized I had finally surrendered to the years of pain and torture I had put myself and so many other good people through. I surrendered to the idea of never being able to drink like a "normal" person. Surrendered to the idea I had any sort of ability to have power over alcohol. And finally surrendered my life to the very Power that created me.

I would love to tell you that I found myself on "Easy Street," but that would be a lie. There was much work to do. God was cleaning my mind and soul. He still is.

Tremendous power comes from surrender.

I have the insane ability to take something simple and complicate the crap out of it. I will play the tapes over and over in my head about how to control a situation or do this or that to fix a problem, and invariably end up finding myself having to surrender.

For more than sixteen years, I have meditated every single morning. I will be late to a meeting rather than skip my morning meditation. I read a quote from Dr. Wayne Dyer many years ago about meditation. He said that when we pray, we are talking to God, and when we meditate, we are listening to God. That made so much sense to me.

Any time I have an important decision to make—any time there is an urgent need or adjustment to make in my goals or life—I ask God for direction. Then, I meditate. One hundred percent of the time, the answers show up.

In the past, I would ask for the answer and it wouldn't appear immediately, so I would give up on the idea and move on to the next thing. Then somewhere down the road, the answer would appear or even be delivered to me. It always has perplexed me. Then I discovered the most important part—the *gestation period*. Is it reasonable to plant a seed and expect the harvest in the next moment? Everything in life has a gestation period.

I've realized if I want more, I must plant more. If I want more love, I must give more love. If I want more attention, I must give more attention. God always delivers based on our level of trust and faith. The solution might not appear in my time; it will more than likely be in His time.

My relationships today are deep. I no longer look at people and think, "What can they do for me?" I see people as extensions of me, as extensions of God. We are One. We are all the same. We may have different skin tones, levels of understanding, or varying degrees of consciousness—but in the end, we are all the same. We all are born into this world with a great purpose, and eventually we all leave this world.

The cool part is: We get to decide how we want to leave this world. We can leave it a better place because we gave it our very best, or we can leave it having made little to no impact at all. That choice is up to us.

Today, I plan my plans. And they are big plans. But I let God handle the results. I surrender.

Awakened

by Helen Heinmiller

I am happy and at peace with myself.

It took me a long time to climb the ladder of success, but I managed to scale the last few greased-up rungs, despite the good-ole-boy protests at my company. I knew I'd made it the day it was approved for me to be part of the team being jetted from Virginia to Boston by our biggest vendor, for a tour by their VP and other elites.

I sat in the cabin of the Cessna, next to a platter of shrimp, fruit, and cheese, pinching myself. Of course, I thought what every other working man would have to think in that situation.

Would my daughter survive without me for a night? Did I bring the right outfits? What if my stockings ran? What if my nervous stomach started up? Could I pull off representing my company well enough to please my super-contentious director, who thought that, as a woman, I was too boisterous at times?"

None of this mattered, because I was living the American Pepto Bismol, Ibuprofen-filled Dream and was a great success in the eyes of many people. So how come I felt the urgent need to run for the hills? This was what I had been working for my whole life!

I found solace in a church prayer group.

Being the working mom of a high-maintenance little girl, combined with a high-pressure job, was harder than I could have imagined. After the trip, I joined a Tuesday night prayer group at our church, hoping for support.

Four women much older than me usually attended the prayer group. The age difference didn't matter to me, because they were so kind and reassuring, like four quirky grandmothers fussing over me for two hours each week.

To my shocked ears, I discovered one of them spoke in tongues.

The first time she did it, my whole body freaked out, and jabs of nerves stung my stomach. Everyone else sat perfectly still with eyes closed, as if nothing strange was going on. After we were done praying, they all looked at me with warm smiles, waiting for my questions. With each loving gaze, my nerves settled down until a shy laugh came out of me.

"What the heck was that?" I asked.

"Jodi speaks in tongues for us. We have someone who can interpret the language, but she doesn't come much anymore," one of the women replied.

I stood there, silent for a moment. Suddenly, a warmth washed over me, making me fully relax. Something about this group of women made me trust them. I could accept that they were different and special.

"Would you like us to assist you in receiving the gifts of the Holy Spirit?" Jodi asked me.

She then explained that, as adults, we can re-receive the Sacrament of Confirmation and promise to use the gifts from the Holy Spirit that we receive at that time. As fate would have it, one of the seven gifts was the gift of tongues. But the idea of chanting in tongues was unsettling. I was already weird enough for people, so I declined their loving offer.

Back in my so-called normal life, I had one of the worst weeks at work. My reputation with my top seven vendors was about to be maligned because my director went behind my back to make an unfair deal with one vendor in the group. My director's betrayal felt like a slap in the face. Each night, I came home weary and not sure if it was worth playing the game anymore.

My daughter paid the price by having an impatient mother unable to balance on the tightrope anymore. Why couldn't I just conform to the system and reap the benefits, like everyone around me? I wondered what was happening to me, as my ethical and moral values were in jeopardy.

My spirit was wasting away while a metaphorical knife twisted in my back.

The next Tuesday, I walked into church, where the four grandmothers stood, and asked to be re-received by the Holy Spirit. I have always been more spiritual than religious but felt desperate and couldn't think of anything else to do. They explained that they would stand around me in a circle and cautioned me not to be afraid if I fainted, as most people do. They would catch me and place me gently on the floor.

"Holy crap," I exclaimed to myself. My last thought was, *Please, please don't give me the gift of tongues – anything but tongues!*

As they started praying, they placed their hands lightly on my head. It felt like a lead barbell as I stood there waiting for the lightheadedness to set in. Jodi started chanting, and her eyes almost rolled back in her head. A couple more minutes went by. Nothing happened.

I kept waiting to fall back.

I kept waiting for something divine to happen. The grandmothers dropped their hands and opened their eyes with their familiar, gentle smiles fixed on me. *Oh My God!* I thought. *I didn't pass out! I was rejected by the Holy Spirit! Oh shit, I must be a bad person after all. What do I do now?*

Jodi saw my concern and tried to comfort me.

"It's okay, Honey. Not everyone falls back. That doesn't mean it didn't work. You wait and see. You'll know when your gifts come."

Everyone nodded in agreement, and then we went to the back of the church and shared slices of an amazing, grandma-made cake. I left with a hundred thoughts swirling in my head, feeling disappointed that I still had no answers about what to do. *How desperate am I to think something like this would help me?* I asked myself.

Feeling more defeated than ever, I got into my little Mitsubishi car and began the winding drive home, surrounded by darkness and the tall cornfields that filled the land.

And then it happened. It occurred in the blink of an eye, a nanosecond event that sparked a lifetime of change. A large Lincoln sedan barreled down the road behind me. Its blinding headlights in my rearview and side mirrors felt like a rhinoceros chasing a mouse.

My edginess began to take over and, cursing under my breath, I drove a little faster than usual. Approaching a dangerous curve in the road, I glanced back to see how close the rhino was to me and heard the words that saved my life.

"Deer! Hit the brakes!"

My foot shifted and pressed down hard. The rhino's brakes screeched as I completed the turn. Just a few yards away, smack in the middle of my lane, was a large, female deer frozen like an ice sculpture. My little Mitsubishi would never have stood a chance against it. Time slowed down to almost nothing, as I watched two invisible hands lift the deer up and place it down on the side of the road, moving like a robot in an assembly line.

I passed the deer eerily locking eyes.

At the next bend, I looked behind me and saw the Lincoln's backend swerve and then right itself coming out of the first curve. A few cautious minutes later, I reached my street and pulled to the curb. As the Lincoln raced by, the adrenaline drained from my face and neck.

I closed my eyes and rubbed them, trying to get the blood flowing again. My body began to shake uncontrollably. I felt so grateful for being warned. If I'd hit the deer, whatever was left of my car would have been demolished by the Lincoln. Turning to thank my passenger, I stared at an empty seat and remembered I was alone.

Stunned, I relived those few seconds, remembering how clear the female voice was that yelled out. I remembered feeling the presence of a passenger in that seat. The voice was loud, and it came from outside my right ear. I even thought I felt a hand grasp my shoulder when it happened.

It took me a few more minutes to put the car in drive and continue home. My husband knew immediately by the look on my face that something had happened. I wasn't sure if I should tell him. Maybe I was having a mental breakdown from the stress at work. As my thoughts reeled in my head, I heard the voice again.

"It's time to write," she said.

For years, I had secretly dreamed of becoming an author. I had taken several writing courses but was always too busy to commit to such a big endeavor. How did this mysterious voice know I wanted to write?

I looked up at my husband and started to cry. I told him everything that happened, including being torn about what I wanted to do. He was supportive but didn't have any answers, either.

At work the next day, I was still trying to process the events of the night before—my miracle, or at least some kind of supernatural event. I had read stories about this type of encounter, but never considered whether they were real. The memory of feeling the presence of a person beside me in the car haunted me the most. *Would this keep happening? Should I fear it? How will this change my life?*

One thing changed almost immediately: My work became more miserable than ever. Everything seemed amplified. Every incident or interaction with management felt harder to deal with now. The company's lack of ethics became obvious and painful to tolerate.

For eight hours a day, it felt like someone was following me around, dragging their screeching nails across a chalkboard. When I challenged the other managers, the writing was on the wall. They were never going to change, and I couldn't continue to work in this environment.

It was crazy to entertain the idea of leaving such a great job, especially for me, without a college degree. The money was good, and we needed my salary to live where we were. But I knew if I stayed, *I would become them someday.* Something greater in me began to rise into my consciousness—a knowing that everything was going to be alright, despite how it looked right now.

Finally. My answer.

I remember the day I left. Hearing a rumor that the Inventory Manager was going to be fired, I turned to my computer and started typing my resignation letter. This manager was a great guy, and his wife was just laid off from her job. He also had a daughter in college. We worked well together, and knew they could not fire both of us at the same time. My resignation wouldn't stop his firing, but maybe it would delay it enough for him to find another job. It was the only form of retaliation I had in my pocket.

After I signed the letter, the feeling of an invisible presence returned. My body began to hum as my anxiety melted away. This time, I felt two people standing behind me. They gently took my arms and lifted me from my seat, then guided me to the human resource manager's office and stood by me as I handed him my letter. He was smug, which I expected, but I smiled as I left.

As the supernatural presence faded away, I felt a new strength build in me. After clearing my desk, I left the building and never looked back. The clear, sunny day felt crisper and more refreshing than ever, like stepping into a new world. Experiencing real freedom for the very first time in my life, I was grateful for my invisible support and no longer feared their presence.

After my awakening, a new job became available for my husband. We left Virginia and moved closer to my family to start a new life.

Soon, many more awakenings would shape my life as I peeled away the layers of illusion that had held me back from understanding who I am. I began writing and exploring our enchanting world. My awakening has allowed me to discover the many healing energies and helpers that are around us. I appreciate every part of our multi-dimensional world. Most importantly, I am happy and at peace with myself.

As for the gifts from the Holy Spirit – I received tongues and a few more!

Hole Hearted Living
by Catherine Paour

Every heart has a story ~ every heart has a gift ~ every heart has a
voice ~ every heart has a purpose.

I never knew what I was missing until I was nine years old and got my first pair of eyeglasses. Suddenly, the world looked vivid and clear. I could read the school chalkboard for the first time. Seemed like a miracle! If only I'd known what I was supposed to be seeing all these years!

However, that wasn't the first miracle in my life. My last five decades have been spent unraveling all the layers of my health history until once again, and again, and again, I received clarity.

My birth was a double breech—or as I like to laughingly put it ... butt first!

They didn't turn babies back in 1960 and probably didn't even know my position till my butt surprised the doctor, and my feet got stuck! My mom recalls that both legs were crossed over my left shoulder, and my left arm was tangled underneath them.

My two older brothers had to hold my legs down whenever mom changed me, and I had to wear three to four cloth diapers to keep my legs from springing back up like rubber bands! I didn't walk until I was two years old. In grade school, I was miserable in physical education (PE), wheezed all the time, and often cried when told to run or jump ... and I never knew why.

I always felt like I couldn't breathe, but at the same time thought that was normal, just like seeing fuzzy without glasses until the age of nine. Following several trips to the Emergency Room, at the age of twelve, my diagnosis was asthma and a heart murmur. My high school years were spent passing out after my morning shower, hiding it from my mom, and suffering the humiliation of being in adaptive PE.

Near the end of my junior year, I had the pleasure of wearing a full body cast to correct my scoliosis. I remember lying down in the back seat of our station wagon to go anywhere and leaning against the wall in the classroom, because sitting in the dang cast was impossible. I wore maternity pants over the cast, and the chest felt like fake boobs made of concrete. That was not my idea of how to get my high school crush to notice me or, God forbid, go on a date!

I got married in 1997 and two months later had a Trans Ischemic Attack (TIA), or a mini stroke.

In 1999, I was pregnant and miserable, beyond what appeared to be normal among my friends. Delivery was brutal. I honestly thought my body wouldn't make it.

At the age of forty-two, I was diagnosed with Congestive Heart Failure, but my doctor couldn't figure out why. This frightened me, since

I was the mom of a toddler—but at least I finally had an answer and could learn how to manage the condition.

As time went on, my symptoms got worse: shortness of breath, debilitating edema, my legs felt like concrete pillars, my digestion was horrible, my heart was pounding outside my chest, I had visual disturbances, and I passed out a lot. My heart rate would soar in an instant to nearly 200 beats per minute and that might last for hours. I would often lose my faculties during an episode. Imagine feeling like you just ran a marathon for the first time, but you never even moved!

A couple of years later, I underwent three cardiac ablations, a surgical procedure where they enter the heart through a catheter and cauterize, or burn, the areas in the heart that are misfiring, and also had three cardioversions, or chemically-induced restarts of the heart—all while going through a divorce.

I felt like a regular at the ER and dreaded going through my extensive medical history with each physician. Every doctor, nurse, technician, you name it, said the same thing: "You're so young to have all this going on." My cardiologist couldn't explain the cause of my heart failure, and the pulmonologists were dumbfounded by my severely reduced lung capacity of 52 percent, which was first measured at the age of seventeen.

I thanked God every day for the Handicapped Parking placard eventually issued to me!

Finally, after another decade of constant physical ailments and stress and strain, I begged my cardiologist of the last thirty years to "dig deeper – I simply can't breathe." It was obvious to me that he felt insulted, but I just knew there was something more.

I had annual echocardiograms and was still on an army of heart meds and an occasional stint of having to carry around oxygen with tubes up my nose. I insisted on every diagnostic test imaginable, but they still found nothing —just my debilitating symptoms and feeling fed up. But rather than feeling sorry for myself, I felt sorry for my young son, who had to watch his mom go through so much medical mayhem.

As my son got older, I wanted to put more focus on my health and wellbeing, so I started working with a life coach. I had so many dreams, passions, and projects I wanted to pursue, but needed help to reignite my sparkle! She helped me peel back the layers and asked me one pivotal question: "What gets in the way of you pursuing your dreams?"

I told her exactly what I felt: my lack of energy and stamina. Being a single mom, working full time, and struggling with my health, all I wanted to do was go home after work and plop on the bed. She helped commit to self-care, to stepping out of my comfort zone, and to seeking out a new cardiologist for a second opinion.

The hole in my heart.

Within a week and after one test in the Cardiac Cath Lab, my new kind and lovely young cardiologist came into my recovery room and hesitantly asked me, "Has anyone ever told you that you have a hole in your heart?"

My mom and I were so shocked, all we could do was answer a big, long, drawn-out "Uh… noooooo" with a tone of voice I'd never heard from my mouth before!

The cardiologist drew a picture showing how my good, oxygenated blood was colliding with the unoxygenated blood, and … well, no wonder I felt like crap! She went on to explain that it's called an *atrial septal defect*—a congenital heart defect I was born with and have lived with, undiagnosed—for fifty-five years!

I was almost happy to hear this, but my mind kept questioning. *How could my original cardiologist have missed it?*

She, too, was quite shocked. She ordered a couple of angiograms to assess how much damage there was to the heart and if I was a candidate for open heart surgery to repair it. The hole was huge. Not just any thoracic surgeon could repair it, which meant I'd have to have the surgery far away from home.

But I was really looking forward to a "new normal" and energy for life, with lots of good oxygen, stamina, and wellness, to fully become a woman of purpose and passion! I was excited at the thought of imagining my future, which I thought could include walking, talking, laughing, and breathing all at the same time!

Reflecting on all my years of declining health, I kept thinking to myself, *It would have been really helpful to know that my heart had a giant hole.* Every medical professional I met after that raised their eyebrows and looked shocked to learn that this went undiagnosed for fifty-five years. "How could the cardiologist have missed it?"

The surgeon told me I had an atrial aneurysm. Most holes in the heart are measured in millimeters and can be closed with a mesh plug through a catheter. But he described my hole as "enormous," measuring six-by-three centimeters! He said the septal wall was "basically non-existent." My heart was just one great big "swamp."

I was lucky to still be alive.

He was able to reconstruct my heart and patch the septal wall using the tissue from my pericardium, a membrane that surrounds the heart. I was never afraid and managed to find the funny in every step along the way, so excited to go from feeling crappy to happy with my new heart!

My surgery went well, despite so many hilarities—like having to sterilize my skin and walk to the hospital from a nearby hotel at five a.m.! My parents took pictures of me on life support per my request, and once it was removed, I had everyone laughing.

I really wanted to put makeup on ... but my surgeon told me I had a completely different skin tone then when I came in there. Wow ... my reflection in the mirror was bizarre! My skin was beautiful! Funny what "good" oxygen will do for you! But no one would ever catch me without my lipstick. I was so happy and possibly trying to flirt... I don't know! Maybe I will be able to date someday!

My eighty and eighty-five-year-old parents, who have always run circles around me, were really scared but tried not to show it. I was so grateful that they were able to help me and my son through this. They also helped add to my laughter. After I was discharged from the hospital, I found my dad roaming around my kitchen, looking for a treat. He said he couldn't understand how anyone can have a house without cookies in it! Like, really? You think I've been to the store?

As days of recovery went on, I felt overwhelmed and incapable of anything. I sounded like a beached walrus trying to get out of bed. My body was loaded with tape, from my jugular and neck down to the belly, and a device attached to my sternum provided suction to my chest incision twenty-four/seven. Both arms were completely black from so many IVs.

My two little Yorkies stunk and didn't understand why they couldn't jump on me in bed! My house stunk. I'm sure I stunk, too. My neck was killing me, my pillows sucked, my doorbell didn't work, and we were in the middle of a heat wave. My breathing was shallow, and I didn't have much of an appetite, but kept thinking, *Good. This better help me lose weight!* Thank God for auto bill-pay, remote controls, and my iPhone.

Three weeks later, I ended up back at the hospital with heart failure, tachycardia, oxygen desaturation, A-fib, blood clots, pulmonary edema, and a host of other complications! That turned into a week in the ICU. There was even mention of a heart transplant!

I remained calm and continued to find humor in my experiences.

I was discharged after a week, but had a lot of recovery ahead of me. Weeks later, still not breathing well, I ended up on oxygen again after begging a doctor to test me, despite how good I might have looked! My recovery kept having setbacks and, a few months later, things got worse when I started Cardiac Rehab and broke my tailbone on an exercise machine! I was back to lying down in the back seat of a car and unable to sit, just like forty years ago in my body cast!

My career as a patient is perpetual, having been through thirteen surgeries, and more recently diagnosed with severe sleep apnea, severely deviated septum, restrictive lung defect, digestive disorder, and hypothyroidism, to name a few. Throw in two additional surgeries and a broken leg last month.

Hmm…. I wonder if I'm ready to date yet!

My focus is still on my health and happiness and inspiring others. I still can't breathe well, but not all sick people look crappy. Some of us are really happy! Some say I look great, and that makes me laugh to myself and think, "I'm defective, not dilapidated!"

Every heart has a story … every heart has a gift … every heart has a voice … and every heart has a purpose. But not every heart has a hole. And me and my hole heart have never been happier.

The Light Inside the Dark
by Dr. Bonnie McLean

Every ending offers a new beginning.

It had been several weeks since my boyfriend had moved out of the house we'd shared for almost two years. He'd announced, unexpectedly, that he didn't want to be in our relationship any longer. One hour later, I received a phone call from my aunt telling me that my mother had died in a house fire.

The shock of both events threw me into a state of traumatic dissociation.

Mother and I had never had a close relationship. I was the eldest child of three, and she considered me rebellious. I thought she was critical and controlling. Both she and my father suffered from alcoholism. As she sank deeper into her illness, our relationship became more and more estranged. Her sudden death left me with unresolved feelings and unfinished business.

Dad had died of throat cancer a few years before Mom. I adored my dad as a young girl, although his profession as a physician didn't allow him much time or energy to spend with his children. He was a distant father figure who suffered from severe PTSD from his experiences and injuries in WWII. Somehow, I understood him and accepted him as he was. As his alcoholism took over his life, he became more and more distant from all three of his children. Looking back, I think I became so used to a man being distant and non-affectionate that I just thought that is how men are.

H (yes, that was his name) was a male nurse. He did provide nurturing and made me feel cared for and accepted for who I was. When he said he was moving out, I was caught off-guard. H said he would stay longer to help me get through the shock and grief over my mother's death. He did stay a month, but when I returned from visiting my best friend for Thanksgiving, he had moved out.

Life felt like a blur.

I pulled up to a cheap motel in a less-than-desirable section of Los Angeles, barely noticing my location, and knocked on the door of the room number of a Peruvian healer. Inti was a young man wearing an orange wrap-around cloth, no shirt, and no shoes. He met me at the door. His long, straight, black hair reached to his buttocks. He asked what kind of healing I wanted, and I explained what had happened and how I felt.

"Are you sure you are ready to move on and to end this relationship?" he asked. "Once this is done, it is done."

"Yes, I'm sure."

Standing in the middle of the room with my eyes closed, I could feel as he danced around me rattling and chanting. Branches hit against my skin and he rubbed several things against me. Later, I learned they had been flowers, stones, and an egg.

When he was finished, he put the egg in my hand and instructed me to throw it into a body of water. I took the egg to Santa Monica. It felt very heavy as I carried it out to the end of the pier and threw it over the side. After I threw the egg, I felt relief, as if a heavy weight had been lifted from me and went home with a clear head and a sense of freedom and peace.

Over the next few weeks, H called a few times. He said he missed me and wanted to keep seeing me on the weekends, but not as a live-in girlfriend. I had no problem declining, having been freed from the grief of that relationship. The shock from my mother's death had also been softened, although it still took a while to heal from that.

What helped the most was going to a retreat in the mountains with my meditation teacher. Wong Lo Sensi had relocated to Los Angeles from Malaysia and, along with other acupuncture students, I had been taking classes from him in Taoist meditation.

He conducted several rituals to assist my mother's soul to go to a good place. I felt a deep sense of peace about my mother's death, almost as if I was finally able to have a relationship with her, even though it was from the "other side."

These two experiences catalyzed my twenty-year journey of self-healing.

Twenty years of travels and studies with teachers, healers, and shamans had healed my traumatic childhood experiences; the low self-esteem and co-dependency that had affected my love relationships; and a low-level depression that I had not realized was lying just below the surface until it lifted.

Even though I had been through quite a few years of intense psychotherapy, the shamanic healing somehow went to the required depth to heal me. The psychotherapy certainly helped me understand myself, but it was the shamanic healing that touched my soul and healed my heart.

Traveling in the U.S. and around the world, I studied with healers and teachers of ancient healing practices. My travels took me to Australia, Bali, the rainforest and Andes of Ecuador, Chili, Brazil, the Philippines, Central America, and across North America.

My teachers, especially those in North America, helped me understand how the shamanic journeys had healed me and how to pass this healing on to my own patients. Through my studies with Sandra Ingerman, PhD, I learned about shamanic "soul loss" and "soul retrieval."

"Soul loss," I learned, is a survival mechanism.

When someone is going through a traumatic experience, their "soul" (essence) moves out of the physical body and into the energy world, to protect itself. A traumatic car accident, a rape, a physical attack, or continuous emotional abuse can cause this.

This self-protective mechanism is intended to be temporary; the essence can return to the body after the danger is over. But when the trauma is severe or ongoing, such as in war and domestic violence—or when it occurs during our formative years of gestation to eight years old—it is possible that not all of our "soul parts" return.

When this happens, a person continues to feel "not quite themselves," perhaps not totally present, or sometimes depressed. They may feel as if they are observing themselves from some place outside their bodies. The role of the shaman is to travel into the energy world they call *non-ordinary reality* and retrieve the "soul parts" that are ready to return. This is usually a process that happens over time, but eventually, the person can feel whole and present once again. This was certainly what happened with me.

My studies with the Foundation for Shamanic Studies helped me understand how the healing I had received from my indigenous healers, including Inti, worked. Dr. Michael Harner, PhD, the founder of this organization, was a psychologist who traveled to different shamanic cultures around the world. He found that, regardless the culture, shamanic healers used the same practices. He called this "core shamanism."

First, there is an invocation to ask the "helping spirits" to be present and to ask them for help for a specific problem. Then they go into an altered state so they can travel into the energy world. Depending on the culture, this is achieved through drumming, rattling, dancing, hitting sticks together, playing an instrument, and chanting. Next, they cleanse the energy body of the client, cutting energy cords and removing blockages to the clients healing process. Fire, water, burning sage and incense, branches, stones, and sometimes an egg might be employed.

Following this ritual, the client's life force and "soul parts" are visualized and blown back into their body. The ceremony concludes by giving thanks for the help of the compassionate spirits and the client's soul for the healing.

Through their open hearts, mine was able to open.

I am grateful to all of the healers and the ancient healing practices that reached the part of me that traditional psychotherapy had not been able to touch: my heart and soul. I now share their healing work in my practice of Chinese Medicine. Like all healers, I work best with patients with whom I have a common experience. In my case, this is trauma.

My own experiences have taught me that healing is rarely a dramatic change. It is subtle. It is incremental. Like the ocean waves, there is an ebb and flow, perhaps two steps forward and one step back. I have also learned that we are our own healers.

We don't, however, heal alone. Healing is much more effective in an environment of unconditional love. It is easier to learn to accept ourselves if we feel accepted. We heal best in community.

I bless each and every "step backward" I have taken in my life. Each apparent setback has been a valuable learning experience and has opened the door to something new and good. I have learned, through all of my experiences that Light can always be found in the dark. Every ending offers a new beginning.

My losses have taught me to live my life in a place of gratitude—for my healers and teachers, for everyone who touches my life, and for life itself.

You. You're Missing You
by Lynn Reilly

I knew to truly feel love from another, I first had to feel it for myself.

I sat on my front porch, sobbing, my heart completely broken into pieces. The pangs of loss were fierce. The grief from the past few years flooded through me—a lifetime of emotion. The huge wave of pain, overpowering and devastatingly harsh, felt all too familiar.

"Why is this happening to me?" I questioned. "What was I missing?"

And then the little voice piped in. You know the one. The one that always seems to know the answers.

"You. You're missing you."

"You've spent your life focusing on everyone else. It's time to focus on you."

My tears began to slow down. Unsure what it meant—but intrigued—I asked for more answers. They came.

"Learn how to love you. Reconnect with yourself. Love and accept who you are, and the rest will fall into place."

It sounded good, but I wasn't sure I knew how. My feelings of being disconnected, lost, sad, lonely, angry, confused, and lots of other downer words could fill up a page. But there was some truth to those statements about self-love and acceptance. And I wanted to learn how to do it.

I again asked that voice to speak up. "Tell me what to do!" I demanded.

I could have been a little gentler, but I was feeling impatient, and it's not my nature to appreciate waiting.

The inspiration came quickly. I knew exactly how to love and support others; that's what I did best. Now it was time for me to learn how to love and support myself.

And it had to be *enjoyable*. No more of this tortured stuff. I needed to treat myself as a priority, with the attention I was craving. With determination, my next steps would be to create a new habit—the habit of taking care of myself, my needs, my priorities—and to try something new.

My pattern of putting others first began as a young child.

My mother had her first "episode," as my father called them, when I was nine months old. "Episode" was defined as an emotional breakdown when she could no longer cope with the stressors of her life. My mother had bouts of delusion, disoriented states, debilitating depression, and highs interspersed between the lows. Her initial diagnosis was paranoid schizophrenia, and she later received a diagnosis of and treatment for manic depression—or as it is now known, bipolar disorder.

My childhood was spent watching my mother ride the waves of excessive highs and deep, disturbing lows. She made various suicide attempts and spent many dark days in her room trying to will herself out of her sorrow-filled emotional instability.

Innately sensitive and an eager listener, I became her confidante. She referred to me as her "little psychiatrist," as I continuously attempted to help her work her way out of her profoundly depressed state.

I recall skipping school often and pretending to be ill to stay home with my mother. Because of my ongoing sense of responsibility, her safety and well-being worried me. She did not do well on her own.

During adolescence, my parents separated and divorced, and I began to grow weary of the need to take care of my mother. I desired to be a normal kid with kid problems and adolescent drama, and did my very best to make this happen.

I began to pull away from her as she continued to spiral downward. When she no longer lived with us, it was easier to keep my distance. It was also easier for her to drift further toward her demise. After several more episodes and cries for help, my mother took her life, less than a week before my fifteenth birthday. My call to duty for her ended in heartbreak, but it would begin my drive to help others in any way possible.

I was always the person people were drawn to talk with and share their concerns.

It was difficult for me to understand why I felt things so deeply or felt responsible for other people's well-being; I just did. If someone was in need, I felt compelled to be a part of their healing. It was not until later in life that I became aware of the fact that, as a child, I had been an empath—someone who is sensitive enough to experience other people's feelings and often sense their thoughts.

It was no surprise that in college, the field of psychology would be my choice of study. It thrilled me to learn that talking to and listening to people was considered an actual skill. My career in counseling allowed me to put other people first. It was my *job*, so it seemed necessary. However, my personal life followed the same pattern.

I made myself available to all of my friends and would always stop to listen, advise, and support them. My romantic relationships were the same. Yet, when/if they tried to support me, I found myself pulling away.

Didn't they see I had to carry the weight of the world on my own?

During my marriage, the pattern continued, with me being everything for my husband while also being independent. The codependent tendencies, created with my help, started to creep in. After having children, my desire to be more than enough was fierce.

Because of my childhood, I wasn't sure if I knew how to mother, but I put all of my energy, knowledge, and emotion into taking care of my kids. Not only did it seem important, but it also felt like the cultural norm. To be a "good" parent, one must put all of one's focus on the children. I bought into it. And due to my fears, I was determined they would never feel neglected or uncared for. Somehow, I'd find ways to shield them from these human realities.

Going back to work and leaving my daughter during the day for so long created immense guilt for me. My anxiety level was through the roof because of the pressure I put on myself to be perfect at everything. For support, I went to a mental health counselor the year after my daughter was born, to help me stop worrying about getting everything right.

I relaxed a bit when my son was born. Less than two years later, my husband lost his job and began to stay home with our kids. Having him home took some pressure off me to do and be everything for our children. But I still felt like I couldn't do or be enough. Guilt engulfed me when I was not with them.

My days and nights were full of anxiety. I tried to distract myself from my discomfort and the feeling of being small and insignificant. I felt as if I was missing something.

I was unhappy, but didn't know why.

Something was changing inside me, and I couldn't escape it. There was nowhere for me to go. I wasn't even sure who I was becoming underneath this skin of mine, but she wanted to come out and be seen. And that scared me very much.

My husband and I were changing, and we began to disconnect and travel down different paths. I realized we couldn't be married anymore. It was both progressive and heart-wrenching. All that remains now is the devastating memory of the aftermath, for both of us, and our family. I wanted so badly to make it work, but couldn't. My anguish was eating me up. It was time to let the marriage go.

I will never forget the sheer panic I felt when I told my husband I couldn't see us together anymore. It was not at all what I'd signed up for or what I'd planned.

The separation and divorce process were undoubtedly one of the most difficult and painful experiences of my life. Making the decision to let go had been challenging, but following through was even harder. Reality felt beastly, and I couldn't escape it.

I felt incredibly selfish, but I knew it was the best decision for all of us. Divorce was the first of my many decisions during the next couple of years that, selfish or not, were the best choices, despite the pain.

They included leaving one career passion to follow another, letting go of friends who pulled away and no longer supported me, and opening my heart when it wanted to close up. When I started taking leaps of faith in various areas of my life, I was onto something. I felt more alive and had greater clarity, although many of my long-standing patterns were still intact and continued to affect me.

Sitting on my porch, crumbling, shaking, my heart feeling shattered, was my wake-up call and became my opportunity to try something new—to get to know me, my authentic self, the part that was begging to come out. She was ready.

The birth of my new way of being began with committing to listening to my own desires, my own feelings, and my own voice. But first I had to learn what they were. I started to "date" myself, to spend time alone and ask myself the same questions I would ask others whom I wanted to learn more about. I listened to the stories in my head that showed me the patterns I had been playing out repeatedly for years.

I watched my comfortable reactions to chaos and my discomfort with peace.

I saw how my early experiences had impacted all of my relationships. I marveled at my determination to be independent, with an even deeper desire to be unconditionally loved. To truly feel it from another, I first had to feel it for myself.

Years of repressed sadness, anger, and fear came to surface as the darkest parts of myself were revealed. I wanted to push them back down and cover them with the cobwebs of my mental basement; instead, I slowly learned to listen to them as if they were my own children. These hidden parts of me were invited to stay for dinner to tell me the stories they had kept locked behind the walls of my shame. I cried with them, coddled them, and nurtured them in ways I had craved to be loved since I was a little girl.

I became the parent, protector, and friend I'd always wanted.

My deep fear was losing someone I loved. But my bigger fear was to lose myself to gain another. Now I love me far too much to let her go again.

Self-love and acceptance are a practice, a daily commitment to show up for myself and pay attention to what I long ignored. It is important to me to be who I am for the sake of my own happiness, and also to inspire my children to live with the courage and pride of being the real them.

This is the legacy I came here for.

A Topsy-Turvy Life of Love
by Maria Lehtman

My compass in life points me to love.

The one common denominator I share with people around the world is that our lives are unpredictable. I can try to plan my life ahead and connect the dots, but in a single moment in time, life will burst open the doors and windows to reality. The Universe, in its great wisdom, will not let me become complacent. I need to learn, and learning happens through trial and error.

My life went completely topsy-turvy in 2017.

My husband was recovering from an accident with a bad injury to his right leg. His pain barely allowed him to walk, let alone work. I felt sad for him; a tall, proud man with a sporty gait, now hindered by a long, titanium plate attached to his right leg. Coupled with my chronic health issues and several challenges in our family, I thought that should have been enough trials for one year. How wrong I was!

September came with the colorful leaves decorating our beautiful Nordic woodlands, the night sky illuminated by a brilliant moon. While photographing the beautiful fall season, the Universe suddenly stepped in. "Hold onto your hats!" I would have said, had I realized what was about to happen to me.

Monday morning, I caught a mild cold. Four days later, my illness had escalated to full-blown pneumonia with blood poisoning. Suddenly, I was barely alive, with minimal oxygen intake. The medical staff recorded in awe that, despite my condition, I had been standing outdoors waiting for the ambulance and "had climbed in by myself with a packed hospital bag." I guess I knew on some unconscious level that I would be staying a while.

When told this later, I remember absolutely nothing of the events surrounding that day, although it did sound like me—stubborn to the end! We have a saying in Finland that we (Finns) push through grey stone if needed. Apparently, that is an accurate description.

After I arrived at the hospital, I was rushed to the Intensive Care Unit (ICU) and in less than two hours, placed under a medically induced coma. While my physical body was lying in the hospital bed with respiratory devices and tubes, my mind was busy roaming through the shadow world of a near-death experience (NDE).

Why do we hold onto life?

I am standing by a mountain river. The water runs muddy, as if someone has spilled oil into it from the source high up in the mountain range. I find the color repulsive. I look at my hands and call out for two wands. Holding a neon-colored, tube-like object in each hand, I declare, "I will now clean the river" and throw the wands into the bubbling, black stream. In a matter of seconds, the water begins to cleanse itself until the whole river is crystal clear. I can see fish and colorful stones at the bottom. Relieved, I turn to continue my healing journey in the long, coma- induced dream.

Ever since I was a child, I kept a dream journal and studied dream analysis and interpretation. I never realized how far my dreaming skills and capabilities would be tested until those weeks in the hospital when I was cast from one mission to another in my NDE shadow world.

While dreaming, I could feel my body. It was hot and freezing. Every cell seemed to ache with the endless pain and difficulty of breathing. Even today, when I cough, my husband turns to me with a worried look and pushes a teacup into my hand, asking if I am okay.

With both of my worlds—the physical and the coma-dream world—filled with pain and infiltrated by shadows, what was it that kept me here on Earth?

Love kept me here.

Love kept me battling to clear the darkness away, even when it seemed utterly hopeless. The Universe of Light is on The Other Side. Desperately homesick, I was ready to throw in my towel and "go home." But I never did.

Time became almost irrelevant as I fought for my life. They say angels are not in a hurry because, for them, life is timeless. But to my body, time was of the essence. I was burning daylight hours lying in a coma. In my heart, none of that mattered. My one quest was to hold onto the ones I loved beyond all physical boundaries. I focused on that from my shadow world.

No matter how much pain was inflicted on me, I had something more substantial. Love! It was embedded into my physical existence. In the lucid dreaming stages, I kept working my way toward my family— my mother, sisters, nieces, and nephews. But, most of all, I sought after my life's most significant grounding force: my husband.

What went through my mind during that coma? Questions! How could I make the people I most loved bereft with loss if I died? How could I leave before my mother, who was still fighting for her life despite all odds? Who would look after my husband? Who was going to be his mortal guardian-angel in the night?

My mind shifted gears. Instead of being filled with fear and despair, I decided to throw everything I had left into the fight and let love and hope conquer all. Slowly, I fought my way back home until one day, I woke up perplexed to realize that one and a half weeks had gone by as quickly as a nap.

Several days later, I was released from ICU to another department. The nurse who tended me said, with a twinkle in her eye, that I was such a fighter, I could come back and work in the ICU with them any time I wanted.

And then, united with my love, we lived happily ever after....

You did not believe that, did you?

You are right. A few days later, I finally returned home with enough strength to take a shower, although I still needed a stroller to get to the end of the street. I looked like a little straw figurine, barely able to stand in the wind. What was my reaction to the Universe? Gratitude? No!

Like someone who returns from a war zone, my mind was partly numb and traumatized, trying to comprehend what had happened. I managed the post-traumatic stress disorder (PTSD) through prayer, emotional support from my husband and a friend, and pure willpower. I needed medications to eat and boost my immune system.

Emotionally, I was filled with complete and utter anger at the Universe.

I had fought my chronic conditions for years, only to be thrown into the netherworlds and pulled back again, physically incapable of thoroughly taking care of myself.

I said to the Universe, "Remember, you kept me here, now let me fully return to life. My family needs me, so you better let me recover. I did my mission. Now it's your turn!"

I became like the Viking in stories and films: utterly fearless and not caring if the skies threw hail or meteors my way. I would have just stood there and said, "Do your worst! You didn't get me the last time—so good luck trying this time!"

Feeling so weak and challenging fate was an odd and hilarious feeling.

After four months, my anger faded.

I calmed down but was still tough and fearless enough to return to working from home. My husband was waiting for another surgery on his leg to remove the titanium plate, and I did not want to put us at financial risk. I cared, so I worked. And perhaps working would take my mind off the nightmares that still haunted me.

After my coma experience, I had more questions about life and death than answers, but I knew one thing for certain: I had lived through one of the toughest missions on my soul's sacred contract for mortal life.

I have always pondered the discussions around the pursuit of happiness.

Today's social media and online self-portraits make it seem as if everything we feel internally needs to be reflected externally. We might feel that, unless we are glowing with an angelic radiance, something is missing in our universal gratitude, abundance, happiness, and peace. Or vice versa—if you look too good, you cannot be sick or unhappy.

I believe we all have our own paths. We have our soul's contracts and sacred bonds that were created long before we ever got here. They define who we are here. As far as I can tell, nowhere did the contract say, "You shall always be happy and completely confident in yourself."

What it most likely did say is, "You shall always have a possibility to connect to Universal and unconditional love. You shall never have to endure your experiences all alone."

I have learned that love has many faces, dimensions, properties, and virtues. Without love, I don't think we can be completely happy. However, we can love without being completely happy. What? Why is that?

The blessing I received from my trial of struggling from despair to hope was learning more patience to love. I suffer and react physically when people treat each other ill. My mind separates feelings through universal love. "Patience," it says, "patience. Love shall prevail."

So then, did she live happily ever after?

I'll tell you what—one day I will. Today I feel incredibly blessed. Love brought me back from the arms of death. That love sustains me in a way only a few people can understand, in the full spectrum of life. And because of that, I am happy.

Final Thoughts

The main thread of wisdom woven throughout the stories in this section can be summed up in the words; "To be in pain is human, but to suffer is a choice." Some of the stories explain how pain might not be a pleasurable experience itself, but it builds pleasure in ways that pleasure alone simply cannot achieve.[1]

The authors of these stories chose not to suffer. Whether born with health challenges, receiving unfavorable health news, or helping others suffering from Covid-19, as did nurse Diane Vich, wellness goes beyond physicality. Health is often a state of inner being and, like beauty, is in the eyes of the beholder, as Catherine Paour told us in *Hole Hearted Living*.

The growing pains of love can be a double-edged sword that brings about a higher level of soul discovery and emotional wellness, as we learned in *The Light Inside the Dark* by Bonnie McLean. Relationships can affect our health. Or the stress we experience can be the beginning of a shift into becoming *Awakened* as described by author Helen Heinmiller.

In this section, no one stood alone during their darkest hours. Someone stood with them. As it did in *Crazy Little Thing Called Love,* surrendering to a Higher Power played a big part in most of the stories. In *Power through Surrender,* Ken Walls shows us how letting go can be more complicated than holding onto unhealthy habits and addictions. But, if we do not let go of what does not work, we cannot embrace a healthy future full of joy.

The healthy relationships we build in life can help us during times of grief, as seen in the next section: *Grief and Loss: Let the Circle Be Unbroken.*

PART 3

GRIEF AND LOSS
Let the Circle Be Unbroken

And in the next step, the struggle lessens.

Dreams of Grief and Love
by Kathleen O'Keefe-Kanavos

Love takes us back but, dreams take us forward.

The phone call came as a shock. "Linda died last night peacefully in her bed at home. We will be holding a service for her in Boston. I'll send you the link to the online page where friends are sharing memories," Linda's husband said. His grief spoke louder than his barely audible words.

I sat down to catch my breath and cradled the phone close to my ear while rocking back and forth in the chair to calm myself. How was this possible? *How could Linda be dead?* She was so young, much too young to die, even from a rare form of Leukemia.

Memories flooded my mind of us as Happy Hour, martini-drinking tennis partners in matching Lululemon skirts. The memories shifted to how she had never ridden a horse until we rode through the Indian Reservations in Palm Springs. She could hardly walk when she got off the horse and could not put her knees together. We laughed so hard, she was afraid she would wet her pants. And, between my cancer treatments, our families vacationed together at exotic resorts in the British West Indies. Linda was always there for me.

Guilt engulfed me. She was my support system during all three of my breast cancers, yet her bone marrow transplant required her to be quarantined. Even her own family could not be with her. I had to focus on more happy times we shared together or be reduced to a puddle of tears on the kitchen floor.

"What if my wig slips over my eye while serving?" I joked to the opposing team across the net. We were tennis partners, but I had to play tennis in a wig. We all laughed. Linda had worked hard to help me find my joy in socializing again.

We would never laugh together again. It seemed impossible.

Linda was dead, and a piece of my heart had died, too.

Although the days after her death turned into weeks and then months, my longing to see Linda again became all-consuming. Her permanent disappearance from my daily life was physically painful. I could not even call her family to see how she was doing. She was gone!

Our relationship had become a life-habit, and breaking it triggered emotional withdrawal. My disbelief was still covering and suffocating me like a heavy, wet blanket. There was no doubt about it: I was a creature of habit, and my grief was not dissipating.

Was Linda happier now? Did she miss me, too? Heck, did she even remember me—or do we forget everyone we loved on earth when we return to heaven?

Desperate for answers, I set a dream intention to see Linda again.

I wrote my dream intention across the top of the page in my dream journal in big, bold letters. Then I read it aloud to myself. Hopefully, my eyes, the windows to my soul, would observe the plan and relay it to my higher self. Placing the journal on the nightstand beside my bed, I turned off the light and climbed between the sheets—and waited to see what would happen.

My breathing became my focus. I began to spin and entered a hypnogogic dream state, flooded with psychedelic colors and the sound of swarming bees.

I was falling through the invisible, mystical dream doors....

People hurried past me on cobblestone city streets lined with gas lamps. It was a warm, beautiful day. The place felt vaguely familiar. During the dream, Linda walked up to me from the bustling crowd and said, "Wanna get a drink?" Her blond hair was radiant in the sunlight.

The question felt so natural, it did not wake me. I followed her. We entered a restaurant with a stylish bar, and after being led to a raised, high-backed booth, we sat side-by-side and ordered martinis while we laughed and chatted ... just like old times. But when our martinis arrived, Linda's martini only had thinly sliced carrots and celery in the glass and no liquid.

"Where is the vodka?" I asked her.

"Oh, I don't drink anymore," she said, "but I wanted to see you, too."

Linda's statement about not drinking was so out of the ordinary, it woke me from my dream.

Linda, the Queen of Martinis, not drinking anymore? The dream was so real, it stayed with me for days. When my husband and I had dinner with Linda's husband a few weeks later, I shared it with him.

He listened intently and then said, "Linda had given up drinking any alcohol right before she started her treatments, and she never drank again. And it sounds like you were in Boston's Legal Seafood Restaurant at Chestnut Hill. It was one of her favorite places because the bar booths face out over the seating area. Linda loved to people-watch."

All of this was news to me. While she was feeling the effects of her bone marrow transplants and chemotherapy, she was usually sleeping when I called her cell phone to check on her.

When she did answer her cell, she often said, "I'm not in a very good place right now. I hope I feel better tomorrow. Let's talk again then."

Although my thoughts were always with her, our verbal communication had been almost non-existent.

And the part of the dream about being in Legal Seafood rang true, too, for two reasons. She had spent her entire life in Boston and knew all the best places to drink and dine. And in the dream, Linda and I sat side-by-side in a booth that faced the tables in the restaurant—so we could people-watch. It made sense that Legal Seafood would be a favorite place for her, and she would know how to get there.

I, on the other hand, born and raised in Europe, was lost in Boston. The quaint, horse-path cobblestone streets were a navigational nightmare for me. With Boston's Big Dig changing road directions and the one-way streets, even my phone GPS did not help.

Was this a wishful dream or a different reality?

Had Linda's husband just given me validation concerning the authenticity of the dream? My time with Linda in the dream world brought me relief from grief, and I awoke in a state of calm joy.

My memories still take me back to nostalgic times, but my dream of being with Linda moved me forward out of grief. Oh, I do still miss her—but the agony of grief is gone.

Can undying love make the shift from a place of crappy to happy?

I believe it did for me.

Cycle of Life
by Bernie Siegel, MD

We had a love few people will experience.

God told me many years ago, a perfect world is not creation. It is a meaningless magic trick. He said, "I have given you imperfections and crap so you would see the role they play in the creation of all life, like fertilizer does for plants. Then you can live and learn from your experiences."

My wife Bobbie reminded me frequently how to live and learn. Years ago, she made lunch for me every day because my life, as a surgeon, was so unscheduled that I needed to carry a meal with me and eat it whenever I had a few minutes of free time. She would put my lunch in a little red, metal lunch box with the word love printed all over it. I still have it. Inside would be my lunch and a love note from her with drawings of our kids and pets and Xs and Os, symbolizing hugs and kisses.

One day, I had so many emergencies and problems that I was exhausted and didn't get to eat until three in the afternoon. When I lifted out the note from her it said, HOLD ON. My wife was quite intuitive, and I assumed she knew it would be a tough day for me, so I "held on." Her message was perfect. Reading it restored me.

That night when I got home, I thanked her for her intuitive and inspiring note. She asked what I was talking about. I explained that I'd had a difficult day, and her note helped me to hang on and get through all my emergencies.

She said, "It was a big sandwich with a lot of vegetables. I just wanted you to hold on to it."

In the years to follow her notes, when appropriate, said, "This is a two-hand sandwich." But she had made my crappy day a happy day, and we've shared that memory from that moment on.

Bodies die, but spirits and consciousness survive and recycle.

I know from my past-life experience that my wife Bobbie and I were not together for the first time in this life. Bodies die, but our consciousness survives and uses what it learns in its present lifetime to enhance the future lives we all experience. In this life, Bobbie and I were married for sixty-four years. She died two years ago, but she's still very much with me in many mystical and incredible ways.

I got a call from a former patient and mystic two days after my wife's death, saying she had a message from a lovely lady who was an opera singer. My wife's mother was an opera singer! The message was, Bobbie was fine and with family again.

Next, I began finding pennies everywhere. We used to call them Pennies from Heaven, because after my mother's death, I found them everywhere. One of her grandchildren first called them pennies from Heaven.

Where did that kid get that idea? I believe it is true, because the little coins appeared in strange places and in places where I had seen no pennies an hour earlier. I even found them in places pennies would not be lost, like wooded areas around our house. My most significant find was a dime and a penny together, because we were married on the eleventh day of July. I found these coin combinations on store checkout counters and in a bird bath in our yard.

At night, when in bed, I thought I heard her voice. I even sat up one night and asked, "Do you need any help?" before I remembered my wife was dead and couldn't be talking to me. Sometimes I also would hear a sound like you make when blowing out a candle and then feel a breeze on my face. I knew my wife was kissing me good night.

Eight months after she died, I had a heart arrhythmia called fibrillation and went to the local emergency room. Heart problems are not unusual when a loved one dies. I heard them call out to staff, "Put him in room number nine." My wife was born on 9/9. So, I knew she was watching over me.

When they had a hospital bed available the next day, it was in room 819. Eight has meaning, representing a new beginning, so again I knew I'd be okay. My hospital identification number on my wrist band is 8996633 and the case numbers also added up to nine. I've saved the bands for nonbelievers to see as evidence.

My wife was born 9/9 and we were married 7/11. This last Mother's Day weekend was a 9 for Saturday, 10 for Sunday, and 11 for Monday. On the ninth of May, I found a dime and a penny in the clothes dryer when I went to take the dry items out. Nothing in the dryer had any chance of having coins in it.

On Sunday, I was making the bed after getting up and went around to the side my wife used to sleep on, to tighten the sheets and blankets by pulling them back. When I lifted them to pull, they felt like they were pulled out of my hands and thrown to the other side of the bed—and what did I see? Yes, a dime and a penny on the bedsheet. I put all the coins in a little plastic bag I keep with my wife's photo in the shirt pocket next to my heart.

Last but not least, the most remarkable event. I wear three rings. One was made by one of our children; it is my family ring. Another made by a patient and friend, and that's my friendship ring. The third is my wedding ring. When I go to sleep at night, I put the rings and my watch in a drawer.

After Bobbie's death, some women who were old friends began to show interest in me, though I was not interested in them. One morning, I looked in the drawer and my friendship ring was missing. There was no sensible explanation for that. Yes, I looked on the floor and all around, but discovered nothing. I felt it was my wife's way of saying, "Stop this stuff with the female friends."

I made sure I did, but no ring appeared for several months. Then one morning while the bedroom carpet was being vacuumed, there on the floor—in plain view—was the ring.

Now back to the latest Mother's Day weekend. On Monday, I opened the drawer, and the friendship ring was missing again. I searched everywhere with a flashlight to see if I might have dropped it under the bed when I put it in the drawer. Nothing found. Two evenings later, as I was getting ready for bed, there on the carpet was the ring—in plain view for anyone to see.

Life is a cycle.

There is no rational explanation for any of these events except that my wife's spirit and consciousness are ever present and still participating in my life and our relationship. We shared a love few people will ever experience. We were like one person when together. I know she is still there, with and for me and our family.

Here is a final test to see if you need Crap Therapy, courtesy of Bobbie Siegel's past efforts to help others:

1. Your husband calls and wants to have dinner out tonight. So, you leave a sandwich on the front porch.

2. You put your bra on backwards and it fits better.

3. You get your hair done and when you get home your dog growls and won't let you in.

4. You call your answering service, and no one answers.

5. You call suicide prevention and they put you on hold.

6. You call the missing persons bureau and they tell you to get lost.

7. You tell your psychiatrist no one is paying attention to you and he says, "Next patient please."

8. You open a fortune cookie and find a summons.

9. You go to a gypsy fortune teller and she offers you a refund.

10. The bird sitting outside your window is a vulture.

Bobbie would remind me, "You can always serve as a bad example." With her help, I've learned not to let sorrow take control and destroy my life. Death is like a commencement, not an ending to our existence.

Know that your loved ones are still there, watching over you and desiring that you continue to find happiness and meaning in your life.

The Little Things
by Constance Bramer

It's the little things in life that you remember:
the ways in which you felt important and loved.

When I was three years old, my mother enrolled me in a ballet class. I was definitely the shortest little girl at the barre, wearing a black leotard, tights, and pink ballet slippers. This was the first of many things my mother did for me that shaped my life.

We began a special tradition.

Starting when I was nine years old, every summer we would go see the New York City Ballet at Saratoga Performing Arts Center in Saratoga Springs. Accompanied by my friend from ballet class and her mom, we would enjoy a fabulous lunch at Lillian's and afterward, walk to a local shop that had Godiva chocolates in a big, beautiful brass case. It was a big deal to pick a single piece of delicious chocolate at the shop. I always picked the milk chocolate hazelnut oyster. It was heavenly. To this day, the taste of hazelnut brings me back to those wonderful moments with my mom.

My mother had a penchant for baking, shopping, and chocolate. The latter started long before our Godiva chocolate days. As for baking, my mother would bake *every* Saturday morning. Chocolate chip cookies were her specialty. She didn't miss many Saturdays, no matter what. Every time she baked, she would leave a glob of chocolate chip cookie dough for my brother and me. She was always thoughtful. Always.

She loved to shop and of course, much to the chagrin of my Visa, I inherited the same zest for sales. We lived in a rural area about an hour from a mall. So, when we went shopping, *we went shopping!* It was a game my mom and I played well.

These were special times I had with my mom that no one can ever take from me, times for which I am incredibly grateful.

My mother was diagnosed with breast cancer when she was forty-six years old.

I was nineteen and in college at the time. It was devastating and yet, she told me she had been expecting it. You see, she was the third generation in her family to be diagnosed with this cancer. And I, twenty years later, would become the fourth.

There were few moments over the following seven years when she wasn't battling cancer. The illness hovered over our family like an ominous alien spacecraft that blocked out the light below. But one thing was certain: Cancer did not steal my mother's inner light.

A couple of years after graduating from college, I joined my family business. Working with family can be stressful, but spending time with my mother *every day* was an incredible gift. My father was also grateful because he no longer had a huge phone bill!

One ordinary Friday fall afternoon, my mom came over to my desk and said me, "Con, let's go shopping tomorrow!"

Understand that this was not uncommon—but the day turned out to be one I will always remember. When shopping day came, mom was feeling well—or maybe she wasn't, but she hid it from me. I think she did that many times. I realized years later, as a mother to two young children, I did very much the same when I was in the midst of my own cancer journey. I get it now. As mothers, we are protectors, which means we're fibbers of the truth at times. We just try to keep the peace and maintain normalcy.

Our normalcy was shopping and finding sales.

If it was on sale, surely, it belonged in our closets.

On this particular day, I was on a mission to find boots. After stopping at a few stores, I finally found a pair I liked. They came in brown and in black. I was in a quandary as to which color to buy. I was trying to be smart with my money and not overspend. I went up to the counter with the black pair, thinking I would be able to wear them with more. As I was checking out, my mother came up behind me with the brown boots. She also had two pairs of shoes for herself.

I looked at her holding the boots and said, "Mom, I'm going to just get the black ones."

"Then I will buy you the brown ones."

"Mom, really, it's okay. I only need the black ones."

She looked me square in the face and, with the clerk standing there at the counter listening to us, she said, "Fuck it. It's only money."

I was shocked. One, that she said the "F word" and two, that she said it in front of a clerk! My mom might have been a saint, but she did occasionally throw a few swear words out there. Using the F word in public, however, was a rare event.

We left that store with our new footwear, took them out to the car, and returned to the mall for some more shopping. My mom perused every sale rack and bought lots of summer dresses that day.

"Stocking up for next year," she said.

It's the little things in life that you remember: the ways in which you felt important and loved.

I remember the drive home and how we laughed and listened to the radio. I had my own apartment about thirty minutes away, but that night, I stayed at my parents' house. I went down to my room when we returned from shopping and found fresh flowers next to my bed. I wondered when she'd had the time to get them.

When I was in college, every time I came home, my mother had a vase of fresh flowers from the local florist waiting for me on my nightstand. She always wanted me to feel special. My mom was gifted in her ability to make others feel this way, too. I was so lucky to be her daughter.

I walked back upstairs to the kitchen to find my mom sitting at the kitchen table in "her" seat with a cup of tea. We had eaten a late lunch at the mall in the food court and we weren't yet hungry for dinner, but we were always ready for chocolate. My favorite Girl Scout cookies are Tagalongs. Mom had designated a shelf in the pantry for me and one for my brother where she would stash our favorite treats. She told me to look on my shelf. I opened the pantry door and there was an unopened box of Tagalongs. Mom and I sat at the kitchen table, talked for hours, and ate the entire box.

If you ask me what we talked about, I couldn't tell you all of the specifics. We talked about anything and everything. But mostly, we laughed. Whether she meant to or not, she had a way of imparting wisdom through conversation. She was my best friend—my confidant and keeper of secrets.

Her laugh was nothing short of marvelous.

For years, we had lied to my father about how much things cost when we went shopping. And seriously, we had it down to a science.

Years earlier, Mom had a charge account at a department store. We would go shopping and "put it on the account," and then come home and give my dad the "prices." We couldn't deviate too much from the real cost, so we would tell him what we spent was about 70 percent of the real price.

I remember laughing hysterically about a reversible jacket she had purchased for me that was a little more than $80. This was in the early '80s, and eighty bucks was a lot of money back then. Our thought process was that it was really two jackets because it was reversible. Two jackets for the price of one! We told my dad it was $55.

He looked at us incredulously and said, "Jesus Christ, I can't believe you spent that much money on a coat!"

Meanwhile, my mom and I looked at each other and laughed silently. This went on in our house for years.

Back at the kitchen table, my mom said, "Your father would have had a stroke today shopping with us."

She threw her head back and laughed her signature-infectious laugh. "If he asks, I'll just do the usual."

Thinking about our new purchases, the reversible jacket, and all of the other items over the years, we both laughed because we knew what that meant.

A few months later, my mom's health seriously declined.

That wonderful day was my last day having my mom all to myself when she was feeling well. The cancer spread and she passed away on April 10, 1996. She fought her battle valiantly and with grace, but she lost, nonetheless. She was fifty-three years young.

After my mom's passing, my dad asked me to clean out her closet. There, hung with the price tags still on them, were a bunch of summer dresses my mother had bought the day when we went shopping. At the bottom of her closet sat the two pairs of shoes. She never got to wear the dresses or the shoes, and maybe she knew that she wouldn't.

I thought about her comment, "Fuck it. It's only money," and realized that shopping and spending money was one thing she could control when she was alive. Her cancer, she could not.

I sat on the floor of her closet and cried. It's one thing to lose your mother; it's quite another to look at her belongings, knowing that she will never touch them or wear them, ever again. With tears streaming down my face, I thought of the trips to the ballet, that one special shopping trip, and how much I loved her.

And all these years later, my love for her has never waned. If anything, it is stronger because in her death, we share a kinship greater than mother and daughter. We share a deep understanding of what it means to be a good mother, a friend, and a person who truly cares about people. I learned all of that from my mother, and for that, I am forever grateful.

My mother was an angel on Earth.

That is how I will forever think of her. I will always cherish that special day and all the wonderful memories I have had, especially the joy of being her daughter: a life filled with fresh flowers at her whimsy, Godiva chocolates, a spoonful of chocolate chip cookie dough, and a box of Tagalong cookies filled with memories of love and laughter.

It's Okay to Die
by Dr. Mark Heidt

Real love is the greatest power of all—
even more powerful than death.

"Your wife died this morning."

Without interruption, the surgeon continued. "I know this is a surprise to you, since your wife had successful heart surgery last week and was here in the hospital recovering and ready to go home tomorrow. But this morning, her white blood cell count went off the charts, indicating a severe infection. I had to rush her into surgery to see what the cause was.

"Fortunately, her chest had not fused, so I did not have to cut the bones, and I could go right in. No time was lost, which was important, because when she was put under anesthesia and placed on the operating table, her heart stopped, and she flat-lined—meaning she was dead.

"And I have to tell you, I've been a surgeon for more than forty years and have never done this before. We practiced the procedure in medical school, but only on cadavers. I never thought I would have to do it. It was a feeling of the miraculous as I placed her heart in my one hand and massaged it with the other. As I did, the heart began to beat again. The pulse started, and she was alive.

"I continued the surgery—found what was causing the infection—and she will be fine. Of course, we had to move her to the Intensive Care Unit (ICU). No need to rush over there now. They will need a few hours to get her prepped. Just as after the first operation, she will still be drugged and asleep, and she'll have all sorts of tubes and monitoring equipment attached—but you already know not to be shocked by that scene. If you need to reach me today, here is my cell phone number."

The surgeon was right; I was used to seeing loved ones in the ICU with all the medical paraphernalia hooked to them. But this time, it went to a new level.

After a week passed, my wife was still in a drug-induced state and breathing with the help of a ventilator. Severe heart cases like hers require several weeks of recovery, so they moved her from the ICU to a specialty section known as the Intensive Cardiac Care Unit (ICCU). I was relieved, knowing the medical staff in that unit are all highly experienced in cardiac care, and the equipment is designed for cardiac recovery. After another week had passed, they were able to remove the breathing tube and lessen the drugs so my wife could at least communicate.

Then came the bad news.

When you have a heart attack, part of your body's defensive response is to shut down other vital organs, including the kidneys. A catheter was removing fluid, but her kidneys were not responding and had not restarted. Then the cardiologist came into the room and gave us the news.

"I have to tell you something. There are two things I never want to experience in my life. One is scraping the bone marrow for cancer treatment. The other is dialysis. It's a very painful, horrible procedure. Unfortunately, your wife is not removing enough fluid and will have to do four-hour sessions of dialysis, three times a week, maybe indefinitely."

My wife dutifully began the sessions. By the end of the third session, she'd had enough. In front of me, my adult son, who was visiting, and the attending nurse, she said, "No more. I won't do any more dialysis."

The nurse, in perhaps the all-time worst bedside manner, said, "Very well, but if you don't do the dialysis, you will be dead in about a week—having drowned to death."

My son, usually stoic, broke into tears. This was his first encounter with the reality of death. My wife's sister also did not receive the news well. She told my wife she did not want her to die and encouraged her to do the dialysis. Shortly after, my daughter and grandson, in tears, pleaded for her to do the dialysis—to no avail.

I did not show my anger, thinking how selfish my wife was to deny others the right to see her live and to be with her. The next morning, I asked her about it.

My wife described the dialysis experience this way: "You are awake the entire time, sensing all the blood being removed from your body. Shivering, you turn freezing cold in an open room with other patients in their beds, all undergoing the dialysis, and it feels and looks like a morgue. Finally, you go into shock, and then the unbearable pain kicks in, bringing you to the edge. By the end of the first hour, you pray to have the Rapture or God take you home."

Suffice it to say, dialysis can be brutal. If you know anyone who must do dialysis, be kind to them.

I returned home that night and, in prayer and meditation, considered the matter.

The still, small voice spoke to me, saying, "Do you think you could ever experience pain so intense that, if given a choice to die or continue the pain, you would choose death?"

My answer was, "Yes." If someone were drilling non-stop into my teeth with a hot drill and no Novocain or sedatives, I believe I would choose death.

Having reversed positions, I no longer had negative feelings toward my wife. Instead, I related directly and entirely to her situation and understood her choice.

The next day, I visited my wife in the hospital, kissed her, and said, "My love, it is okay if you die. I love you and will miss you beyond words, and so will our children and grandchildren and family. But I understand. Some pains are so unbearable, death is an acceptable choice. I would have made the same choice. No more dialysis."

She relaxed and took a deep breath, as if the chains of death had been broken.

Knowing I understood her and was giving it my best to relate to her feelings gave my wife permission to make a life/death choice. Knowing I was going to support her decision, she made a different decision.

"If they will do it two days a week for two hours, I will give it my best and see if we can get through this—as long as you know that, if it gets too painful, I will need to stop,"

I told her I agreed and would talk to the doctor.

There is more to the recovery story, but here is the crappy to happy end.

After three months of the two-hour, twice-weekly sessions—and with the care of several angelic nurses, doctors, rehab staff, and nursing facilities—my wife's kidneys began working, and she was taken off dialysis. Six months later, she was fully recovered. Today, if you saw her, you would not suspect she had undergone any surgeries or trauma.

We should value life, our own, and the lives of those important to us. Yes, as Dylan Thomas opined, "We should not go gentle into the night, rather rage against the dying of the light."

But we must not let our love for another, or the pain we would suffer by their passing, become judge, jury, and certainly not the warden of guilt.

Love requires not just understanding but also empathy, reversing positions, walking a few miles in their shoes, and supporting their decision.

To tell another, "It's okay to die," is risky. They might choose death, and you will lose them. But it also provides a key to unlock new possibilities of life. This is because real love is the greatest power of all—even more powerful than death.

When you muster the courage to express genuine love, that love brings forth understanding and peace.

Five Years to Live
by Frank Zaccari

Do not be a spectator in life.

On the evening of August 11, 1985, I received a phone call that anyone would dread. There had been a terrible accident involving my twenty-four-year-old brother Steve. I'd just been with him two days prior, celebrating his engagement and job promotion. Life was as good as it could get. Now I couldn't believe the news I was hearing: Steve was paralyzed.

I tried hard to control the panic building in my mind and body.

"Is he going to die? Is the paralysis permanent? Will he be confined to a wheelchair? What will he be able to do? Will he be able to hold a job? How will he support himself? Will he have to live in a nursing home? How long will he be in the hospital?" I asked of everyone possible at the hospital.

"It is too soon to tell, but he will be transferred to Thomas Jefferson Hospital in Philadelphia, one of the finest spinal cord hospitals in the country. They will call you when he arrives," was their reply.

We could only pray and wait.

There is nothing worse than waiting and not knowing. The fear and uncertainty consume you. Once the surgery was over, the doctor provided the clinical results and set our expectations going forward. As bad as things had been up to this point, they were about to get even worse.

"Surgery was as successful as possible," she said. "However, the damage to the spinal cord is such that Steve will be confined to a wheelchair for the rest of his life."

There was an audible gasp in the room and tears started to flow.

The doctor continued, "He is what we call a *quadriplegic,* since he can move his arms but does not have control over his fingers. He will need constant care. He will not have any control over his bowels and bladder. He will have trouble regulating his body temperature.

"He will likely need additional surgeries. He will struggle with bladder, urinary tract, and kidney infections. His skin will start to break down from poor circulation. Any of these issues can be fatal."

Then the killer statement about life expectancy.

"Many patients with this level of injury die within five years. Many others live longer." The doctor took a deep breath before continuing. "This is a life-changing event for Steve, and for all of you. He is never going to be the same. He will need help dressing and cleaning himself."

The doctor paused for a moment to let us process what she was saying, and then continued, "You might want to consider putting him in a good nursing home."

Reality started to set in.

Everything we knew was gone, but we knew there was no way we were going to put my brother in a nursing home. My family and my brother knew he would have to learn how to perform every basic function in life all over again. Would he have the herculean strength necessary to rebuild his body, his mind, and his life? Would we be able to provide the support and assistance needed?

After several weeks, Steve was transferred to Magee Rehabilitation Center in Philadelphia, which would be his home for several months. Living in California, I felt I could provide little to no value. I arranged a transfer to South Carolina so I could be an hour flight from Philadelphia. Being a large family, we were able to rotate who would be in Philadelphia for support.

Mountains of insurance forms, papers, and statements were completed and submitted into the "black hole" so the health care provider and the worker's compensation carrier could battle it out to see which one would ultimately have to pay. As difficult as the initial trauma and rehabilitation were, dealing with insurance companies was worse. Every call with the insurance company felt like an exercise in futility. They never gave a straight answer. They kept asking and rephrasing questions over and over, hoping for any slight variation or inconsistency. It got to the point where we created our own script to answer their questions.

Sensing we might have a battle with insurance, I secured a law firm in Philadelphia. The last thing the attorney said to me was, "We will make sure he is protected. Direct all the insurance calls to us." This allowed me and my family to relax and turn all our focus to supporting Steve.

I saw two potential role models at Magee.

While these two men while not happy with their situation, they had accepted their new life and were extremely positive every step along the way. When they connected with Steve, we saw his demeanor become more positive. This was a tremendous relief.

After several months at Magee, Steve returned home to Buffalo, NY with a modified van. I felt a tremendous sense of relief knowing he was out of imminent danger, but he still had a long road to return to a productive life.

As I expected, there was a court battle with the insurance company. We won. While none of us could make Steve walk again, we were able to remove as many legal barriers as possible. This allowed us to move from fear and panic to a sense that we were doing something positive.

With the legal, insurance, and equipment issues out of the way, Steve went back to school. He earned a master's degree at Buffalo State University, and then was hired by the State University of New York at Fredonia as an advocate for students with disabilities. He was active in this role and instituted many improvements at the school.

It didn't take long to realize that living in Buffalo's harsh, snowy climate with a power chair was not going to work. My sister Annette, who ran rehabilitation hospitals, had moved to Phoenix. In what seemed like divine intervention, the house next door to hers was suddenly for sale. Steve bought the house. Insurance did the renovations, and the entire family helped him move. He started a new life in Arizona.

With Steve in Arizona, I moved back to California to be close enough to help when needed.

Do not be a spectator in life.

I pray to God that you and your loved ones are never faced with this type of life-altering event, but there are no guarantees in life. Sometimes things appear overwhelming—they are not.

Remember these three things: Look up. Get up. And never, ever give up. You don't know how strong you are until being strong is your only option.

Steve, who was told he might live five years post-accident, is about to celebrate his thirty-fifth anniversary.

An Epic Healing Journey
by Dr. Julie Krull

What more could this moment of grace teach me?

When the courageous and often-*heroic* medical treatments failed after many years, it was time to make a decision. Stay in the hospital until he died, or go home on hospice care. My dad chose to go home.

My three sisters and I went to be with him and our stepmom. Even though his health declined rapidly, that week was a blessed time of love and healing. We took turns staying up with him at night, soaking in the unexpected gifts that came with deepening compassion.

On Valentine's Day, I sat beside his hospital bed at 3:30 a.m. He slept restlessly through the pain in an incoherent state of tolerance. I put my hand on his, and without missing a beat, in his sleep, he whispered, "I love yahz."

He softly winced and moaned, and then became quiet again. In the middle of the family room, he was bundled under layers and layers of blankets, hand-stitched quilts and crocheted throws, with his left foot hanging out of the covers—on purpose.

Perched on a folding chair next to his bed, I was wrapped with my own layers of pajamas, sweater, and vest. We were both warm and cozy, though uncomfortably so, given the circumstances. Through his irregular breathing, wincing, and moaning, whether asleep or lucid, he continued to whisper messages of love: "I love you, oh how I love you." Moans of pain, his cough, and the sweet sound of his love-whispers became a new kind of clock, marking time as it passed in the middle of the night.

He woke himself up, grimacing with a loud noise. I rested my hand on his shoulder, and he quieted down. Gently, the sound of the home oxygen concentrator and the manifest warmth of a strange, loving Presence eased him back to his shallow rest, but not before he sent out more love. "Ahhh . . . I loves ya, Jules."

"I love you too, Dad," I quietly replied.

A beautiful Valentine's Day.

In the darkness, offset by only the dim light of my computer, I reflected on what a beautiful Valentine this was. I was soaking in the bittersweet, merciful blessing of sharing his last hours. I was communing in a grace-filled resonance, even as his breathing created discordant music. This love was infinitely real and deep, though delivered in a delirious container of pain. The benevolence of this otherwise painful moment was so precious.

A whimper, then a loud groan, brought me back into the moment. It was time to roll over. We worked together to find a comfortable position on his left side, propping pillows in the perfect places, and rearranging the covers.

"How's that, Dad?"

"Oh, it's good … it's good until it's not," he said and quietly drifted back into the feverish abyss of his restless reality. I chuckled at his commentary. The whispers, moans, and cough continued into the early morning hours. And time passed.

He woke again with an unpleasant howl, "OH-Oooohhh-OH!" and then quietly said, "I love you, honey."

"I love you too, Dad. Can I get you something for the pain?"

"Oh, no … I'm okay. It hurts more everywhere than anywhere," he answered in his kind, but humorous way. Then he turned to me. "Why don't you go lie down in the recliner and try to get some sleep?"

I replied, "I'm okay, Dad. I'm sitting here writing love letters on my computer."

"Ah . . . that's good! Real, real, good," he replied with enthusiasm. "I LOVE YOU!" he added.

A tear rolled down my cheek. "I know, Dad. I love you too," I whispered in gratitude. And time passed.

As it turned out, that was the beginning of the end. Valentine's Day was his last coherent day. We had a beautiful day of celebration with his favorite meal and lots of tender memories. By eleven p.m., the tide was turning, and the hospice staff arrived around midnight. They coached us as to what to expect and how things would change.

A few hours later, the hospice nurse suggested we say our goodbyes. We entered the end-stage, which usually takes three or four hours. However, our deathbed vigil turned into an epic journey, and we were in the eleventh hour. It was such a long and laborious night for him.

Labor and delivery.

My memory of those moments shortly before my first child was born is keen; I felt like giving up—desperately. Not managing my pain well, I wanted the unbearable process to stop. I literally wanted to quit, pack up, and go home. However, this blessed event was irreversible and forever life changing. There was no stopping the process once it had started. The only way out was through.

Resistance and fear constrict. I have learned that avoiding pain or conflict does not resolve the issue at hand. Both life experience and professional training have encouraged me to get out of my own way and trust the process. The pain of holding back, resisting, and trying to change or control the situation is often greater than the perceived pain of the actual process of being fully engaged and present in the moment. It's almost always best to surrender—to simply let go. As a result, I've become more pliable and resilient.

With the birth of my first child, contractions in my lower back, coupled with my first-time-mom fear of the unknown, made it nearly impossible to relax, do Lamaze breathing, and surrender into the experience of childbirth. After I'd pushed for more than two hours, the doctor finally asserted he was stepping in to use forceps to assist in the delivery. A few minutes later, my son was delivered and took his first breath.

Sitting beside my father's bed, I witnessed his laboring. Cycles of shallow breathing, weakened pulse, and peaceful pauses were interrupted with what seemed like excruciating labor pains. Wincing and moaning, he journeyed through an endless rhythm of contractions as he prepared to leave his body. Then, at the moment when we thought he'd been delivered into the peaceful embrace of death, another wave of un-surrendered life sent him laboring for enough breath to get him through the next contraction.

Flashes of that moment—giving birth so long ago—grabbed my attention. I beheld my father in an arduous dance within the liminal portal—somewhere between life and death (the "death canal," if you will), managing his own labor and delivery.

I recognized myself compassionately sharing his fatigue and resistance. He had labored for hours. Fear of the unknown lingered in the room. I wanted the process to stop! In my own discomfort and pain, I prayed for a quick and easy delivery. I observed myself in the throes of self-induced suffering, not wanting him to suffer.

But like birth, this was, I knew, another one of those blessed events that was irreversible and forever life-changing. And he had to go through it alone. I could choose to experience his death in a limited state—one of fear, separation, resistance, and pain—or I could shift my reality and awareness to open into the expansive, sacred knowing of this most-blessed moment.

I paused, took a deep breath, and tuned-in to the resonant field of love in the room. Calling on my higher self, I quickly discovered a cosmic harmony within the life cycle of birth and death, witnessing this eloquent process and myself within it. The mystical doors of the Universe opened as I experienced tremendous grace and deep meaning in this Holy process.

I found peace.

Instead of the fear, pain, resistance, and suffering that had gripped my attention, I found peace. I was handed a precious gift and consciously chose to claim and receive it. I stepped through my own limiting portal of embodied consciousness and became fully present to the Mystery and miracle of life. Surrendering, I relaxed into the death process and became one with it.

Physical death was my father's lone journey now. We all wanted to be there for him—with him—to support and comfort him in his transition. We desperately desired a peaceful resolution. However, this was his delivery, and only he could labor through the process and move through the transcendent birth/death canal. This was the work of the soul. He had to go through this narrow portal to deliver himself.

The hospice nurse, Lisa, in her palliative wisdom, intuited the same thing as I left the bedside and went to sit in a recliner, several feet away. She kindly invited us to step away and rest in another room for a while, allowing my dad to fully relax into this sacred dying process. We were all there with loving intentions to support him in the transition. Yet our relationships as wife and daughters, perhaps, held him in a place of resistance and emotional attachment or interference, keeping him in his earthly embodiment as husband and father.

It was time for him to release himself and give birth to the celestial role of his greater essence.

Her gentle suggestion was perfect. The short time of physical separation assisted in his ability to relax and surrender. Having us step away allowed a heavenly midwife, with divine forceps, to step in and assist. He let go, moved through the portal, and finally found peace. A few minutes later, my dad was delivered and took his last breath.

My dad birthed himself back into the mystery of his full, divine nature.

I was humbled and honored to participate. After decades exploring the concept of the divine human, the emergence of infinite mind, and as some might say, the embodiment of Christ Consciousness or our Buddha Nature, this tender moment touched me. I have had a perpetual curiosity and passion for bringing spirit more fully into matter and bringing consciousness into life more completely. Yet I had just witnessed my father slip through the ephemeral gateway in reverse. The Holy blueprint was becoming clearer. What more could this moment of grace teach me?

We must say goodbye, grieve, and acknowledge the death that is occurring. The evolution of consciousness and our spiritual awakening is a death/rebirth cycle. Remembering and reclaiming our wholeness is a palpable transfiguration process. As with my father's epic death vigil, I am invited to step aside, trust the Designing Intelligence, and relax into resonance with the higher plan and process. I am dying and I am birthing. Experiencing the liminal space in this new context, I trust in the blessings and gifts, even though I may not see or know them yet.

Allowing. Letting go. Surrendering.

How Losing My Cats Turned Into Blessings

by Ellie Pechet, M.Ed

Mission Impossible Accomplished!

My cats, Blue and Snickers, were high-level beings and two of my most significant soulmates. They both had grown up with a sister-turtle named Ellie Jr., and so I was pleasantly surprised when, after their deaths at age twenty and a half, they resumed their roles as my animal-spirit-guides … and turtles.

They guided me to fulfill my life purpose.

Twenty years ago, I adopted two kittens from a nearby shelter in New Bedford. The female was a charcoal grey Russian Blue and the male was tan, brown, and white with stripes on his face that looked like an artist had drawn them. I named the female Blue and the male Snickers because he reminded me of a Snickers candy bar and truly was oh-so-sweet. I took them home to meet their sister Ellie Jr., the free-spirited turtle.

We all began to communicate telepathically, and I discovered the cats each had a different, specific role. Snickers was the Wise-Professor-Healer and a bit of a goofball. Blue was the Warrior-Queen-Protector.

Life eventually shifted from happy to crappy.

Their twentieth birthday party was an enormous milestone filled with favorites, like tuna fish juice, catnip treats, and lots of brushing. Six months later, Blue developed digestive issues and began to eat less and less. The hospital x-ray showed an abdominal mass.

Blue told me she feared we would lose our connection when she died, so, during a healing session with her, I strengthened the connection between all of our chakras, especially our heart chakras. When it was time to let her go to sleep, I held her gently and whispered loving sentiments as she peacefully drifted away. Then, within about thirty seconds, a little voice over my right shoulder said, "I'm right here, Mommy! I'm okay!" It was music to my ears and that continued in the car all the way home. Huge wow ... she was okay and still with me!

Three months later, Snickers' gingivitis and tooth resorption got so bad he wanted to join his lifelong companion. He told me he had already stayed longer than expected and was grateful for all the healing work I had done on him and Blue over the years, which had prolonged both of their lives for about five years.

When the doctor came back into the room, I wrapped myself around Snickers as he took his last breath. I could feel Blue there with us, ready to help Snickers make the transition.

Losing my beloved companions only three months apart was emotionally devastating.

My blood pressure went up for the first time in my life. Mentally and physically exhausted, I couldn't believe I would not be able to massage them or whisper sweet, loving sentiments in their ears anymore. I didn't think I would ever be able to get over losing them.

Little did I know, they would now become more involved in my life from the "other side." Three months after they reunited in heaven, they began to help me on earth.

One of the essential aspects of the cats' spirit-guide mission was keeping me focused on my life-mission: to expand my remote healing work and advocacy work with animal groups worldwide, such as those affected by the fires in Australia, elephants in Africa, whales in the Atlantic, a group of black bears in North Carolina, and currently, my native neighborhood turtles in Massachusetts.

One day, while driving to the gym, a tiny black object in the road caught my attention.

It was a turtle. May to mid-July is the egg-laying season for turtles, and she was trying to make her way across the road to deposit her eggs. I pulled over, got out of the car, gently picked her up, carried her to the other side of the road where she was headed, putting her down in a spot far from traffic.

A couple of weeks later, I was dismayed to see a dead turtle in the road, run over by a motorist. A closer look revealed this one was a six-inch-long red-eared slider. I felt emotionally crushed. A gorgeous, red-eared slider turtle had been trying her best to cross a bridge and lay precious eggs to continue the cycle of life … and a car stole her life.

I vowed aloud to the lifeless body on the bridge, "I will take action and not allow beautiful beings like you to keep getting run over."

I realized that most local residents were unaware this bridge was a turtle crossing that went over a creek where the turtles lived.

It became my goal to enlighten them.

After parking the car, I walked door-to-door to see if the people in the houses closest to the creek were aware that the bridge was a turtle crossing. The first house belonged to a young family.

"Did you know there is a turtle crossing about a hundred yards from your house?" I asked the puzzled-looking person. They said they had no idea.

"Would you be willing to help me raise awareness about the turtle crossing?"

They said they were too busy. I thanked them for their time and asked them to keep an eye out for turtles when driving over the bridge.

The residents of the next house gave me a similar response. But they did share a beneficial tip concerning a group who was only two blocks away. This group advocated for bodies of water, such as the creek that flowed under the bridge. Surely, they would know this was a turtle crossing. Wrong!

They had no idea and said were also too busy to assist me, but they did share the information of two contacts who might be able to help me: conservationists in each of the two towns where the bridge intersected.

The coronavirus had reduced town government to a skeleton crew. After driving to each town hall and leaving messages for each woman in charge of nature conservation, I drove home.

While I did the legwork, the cats helped from the spirit world.

I am not a political person; I am an energy healer. Getting two towns to agree to install turtle crossing signs on the bridge seemed a bit overwhelming. But my beloved Snickers and Blue stepped in and helped me break down the steps necessary to accomplish our goal.

Blue and Snicker had a connection to these turtles of different sizes and species, (many of whom are endangered) because of Ellie Jr., who telepathically chimed in with suggestions from her pond. We were a family working together from heaven and earth on behalf of the wild turtles.

The cats were with me every step of the way. They assisted by shining a light on all the people necessary to install the signs legally in two different towns. And when I got stuck, they helped me with problem-solving.

One day, while thinking about Ellie Jr., the cats inspired me to Google "turtle crossing" signs. At my own expense, I ordered the ones that appeared to be most effective. My goal was to speed up the process of getting signs posted in time for turtle egg-laying season.

The local newspaper heard about my turtle quest and published a story about my work with the two towns to get turtle crossing signs posted at a spot that spanned both towns. What the newspaper did not know was how or why the cats had their paws in it.

Warrior Blue pushed me to coordinate efforts between the towns to install the signs. At the same time, Professor Snickers got the newspaper story published in time to educate the public and raise awareness for the turtle season. And they both helped the report get republished in other publications.

The result? The counties posted the multi-county signs in time for the egg-laying season.

Mission Impossible Accomplished!

Receiving spirit communication from my cats Snickers and Blue after losing them in physical form is the highest blessing imaginable. We often sit together in the morning, and I can hear them clearly after my meditation and prayers.

I understand now that Blue and Snickers came to me as members of my team of Earth-Angel-Guides in the form of cats. They are so much more than two ordinary cats. They are Animal-Spirit-Guides, helping me even more from beyond the Veil.

We also have something to look forward to. The three of us recently made a plan for Blue and Snickers to return to me as sister and brother black Labrador puppies. They told me they want to live in a house with woods and a big back yard with a fence around it.

For now, the cats are focused on helping me with my life-mission: doing remote healing work with collective groups of animals and the planet.

Search Within

by Deborah J. Beauvais

Go within and discover the gift.

When the soul suffers, the body cries out in pain.

My body screamed when I received the phone call of my husband's unexpected death. A motorcycle accident. There had been no time to prepare. No time for good-byes. Every muscle, nerve, and part of my body ached in physical pain as I dealt with the shock.

For years afterward, it was like a disease I needed to heal but I had no idea how or where to start. Rick's death felt like a nightmare from the darkest place on earth. Yet, it helped me look back at my painful past.

"If you are reading this …"

Rick was an avid motorcyclist and taught motorcycling safety classes. Yet, while on his way to work, a construction truck didn't see him. I'm not at all surprised he "went out" on his motorcycle. At some level, he must have known he was going to leave, because he left letters for me and one for each of his daughters. I have no idea when he wrote them. We found them in a dresser drawer in our bedroom.

He had written, "If you are reading this ..." and told me how much he loved me and would miss me.

For a couple of years after Rick's death, I just went through the motions of life. It was a time when I experienced migraines almost every day. I didn't know a way out. Eventually, holding all the pain inside me caused other organs to falter.

Rick's death triggered memories buried deep in my psyche.

Painful memories about my parents, my tumultuous childhood, and my abusive first marriage surfaced. These memories began to affect my health and parenting.

During the early days of my grief, I told myself my childhood and first marriage had made me suffer more than anyone else. I created a victim mindset and lived from this place for years. Poor me; a life with no loving husband and the big responsibility of raising my three young girls by myself. The job of being a single mother was overwhelming, and I realized the overwhelm stemmed from my childhood memories.

My mom was an amazing parent in the earlier years of my life. She was an excellent cook who also made all our clothes, sewed curtains, did upholstery, and even created our Halloween costumes. But, having had her own tumultuous childhood, she began to change when I was around nine years of age.

Life became too much for my mother.

Back then, no word was ever spoken about what had happened in her life. Her past was swept under the rug, and the cycle of abuse continued with us, her children.

As kids, my sister and I became the mother to our siblings. We did all the chores and then some. We had to learn how to make perfect cocktail drinks for my mom. We experienced and witnessed many uncomfortable things.

At the delicate age of thirteen, my mom abandoned me. She took my younger siblings and, in the dead of night, she left … with another man.

My mother had left my dad, who was a farmer with pigs, cows, and a lot of milk. He worked hard, long hours. He was a good provider but had not been taught love by his parents. Therefore, he did not know how to express himself or show emotion. I loved him dearly in the early days of my childhood and was the catalyst to get him to say "I love you" a few years before his passing, and after Rick's death.

Years later, after my father had crossed over to death, my sister gave me a book to read to help with my grief. The words of love soothed me, and my heart began to open. I realized that, despite being raised in a family without displays of love, I loved my daughters deeply. I also knew my family loved me, despite my fear of abandonment.

At the time, I didn't really have a relationship with my God Source. Joining a religion didn't resonate with me, so I chose to read books. This led to my asking many questions about my life, experiences, and choices. The constant reading launched my healing from the ground level up.

I had to go within myself and listen to my body and thoughts, to learn about my true self.

My healing modalities after Rick's death included Reiki healing, Theta healing, and Past Life Regression. I started to meditate. Initially, I could only keep my mind quiet for five minutes, but I was determined to heal all wounds and feel whole. After a few weeks, I found that if I arched my back with arms stretched out and palms up, I felt more connected to the Universe.

Shortly after doing this, I began to experience tingling in my toes with each meditation. Gradually, the tingles moved through my entire body. Memories surfaced, begging for attention. Each experience included a most glorious light with deep feeling for love and "All that is." I was now having a blessed relationship with my God Source in my own unique way.

Over the next few months, my migraines and physical pain lessened and continued to decrease until they were completely gone. I was elated and in disbelief at how far I had come on my healing journey.

Years later, I had the honor of having Rick for one night after his death.

It was just as real as if he were here with me in the flesh. There have been many endearing messages and dreams to assist me in my healing, but in this case, Rick came through during an energy healing session. The facilitator said, "Rick is here!"

I answered, "Yes, I can feel him." We both felt him physically and heard his message. His appearance allowed me to resonate at a higher frequency for three days. Quite phenomenal!

Death can be devastating for those left behind. Many of us haven't evolved enough as a species to see our deceased loved ones on the other side. But our loved ones aren't that far away. Their blessings and love come from their messages and visits in dreams, meditations, and waking synchronicities with which they gift us.

Searching within propelled me forward into a healthy, joyful life.

One of the many things learned during this long road to health and wellness through grief was to embrace my parents and honor them, despite their treatment of me. My journey helped me discover the meaning of why I allowed myself to be abused in my first marriage.

Everything is woven together in life. The messages that share where to find healing are everywhere. An emotional piece always went along with the physical healing of my body. It was my choice … to go within, embrace any illness, and discover the gift.

The common denominator in the equation of life for me was valuing and loving myself just as I am and freeing myself from feelings of abandonment. I didn't need to carry the heavy load; I could be free, if I allowed my thoughts to focus on love and gratitude. All my experiences on this journey of life could be embraced if I alone made a choice to do so.

I believe life on earth is for healing ourselves, as well as others. We are here to grow our souls by feeling emotions and experiences, even when they are painful.

When I healed, my life became rich with love, gratitude, and humility. Now, I notice the blessings in everything on Earth and can smile.

Final Thoughts

Life and death are the unbroken circle of our existence on earth and the bookends of life. Grief is an expression of love and loss. Without love, there cannot be grief. Many of the stories in this section pointed to something backed by research: Bereavement is often a rite-of-passage that can make the griever emotionally stronger.[1] Grief is an opportunity for significant human experience.

Frank Zaccari and Mark Heidt share how grief can lead us back to our hearts for inner harmony. Unity with our emotions can bring forth innate healing gifts. And death can connect us with ancient wisdom through dreams.

This section brings compassion to the reader as authors share their sacred rite-of-passage. Whether we are the one leaving this world, or the ones left behind, we need support to travel the rushing rivers of emotion that come to claim us. Stories about how to navigate the journey from life to death with joy are a blessing.

Through these emotional stories, the authors bring death and despair back to their sacred places in the beauty, mystery, and celebration of life. It is all part of the next section, *Life Journey and Identity: The Long and Winding Road.*

PART 4

LIFE JOURNEY AND IDENTITY
The Long and Winding Road

What will your sacred story be?

Enough About Me

by Rev. Ariel Patricia

Time for the We.

Flight delayed.

Great. Now I won't get into Salt Lake City until almost midnight, I silently fumed.

Work had been busy, and I almost wasn't going to attend the Parliament of World's Religions, a global event to cultivate harmony and foster engagement among the world's religious and spiritual communities. But since being ordained as an interfaith minister the year before, this was one event I didn't want to miss. When one of my seminary sisters told me about an unexpected cancelation and an opening in her hotel room, I decided it was kismet and made plans to take a quick, two-day trip.

Due to my work schedule, I was already missing the first and last days of the Parliament. Now this unexpected flight delay would make me miss the sessions I'd planned on attending that evening.

Kismet occurs in many forms.

Arriving at the hotel at midnight, I creep into my room as quietly as possible, trying not to wake the woman who'll be my roomie for the next few days. Falling into bed, I set my alarm for six a.m., excited to get up early and participate fully in the day's events.

I jump out of bed full of adrenaline and dash into the bathroom for a quick shower. Fumbling around in the small hotel bathroom, I open a new pair of contact lenses, knowing it will be a long day and not wanting any dryness or irritation from older lenses. But in my eyes, the new contacts begin to hurt and my vision becomes blurry.

Ugh. What's going on? Do I have a bad pair? I wonder.

Not wanting to waste any more time, I take the contacts out, open another new pair, and pop them into my eyes—with the same result. Aching eyes and blurry vision.

"What the heck? This is ridiculous. I don't have time for this," I mutter, taking the contacts out. *I'll just do the best I can without them. I wish I had not left my eyeglasses at home.*

The bane of my existence.

The convention center is only a few blocks away, and I grab a sweater and head out, excited to see Salt Lake City for the first time. Walking down the street, I breathe in the fresh mountain air and say hello to the other early birds who are out and about. Looking up at the mountain peaks in the distance, I smile at their beauty…

Wait, what? I smile at their beauty? How am I seeing their beauty? Their peaks must be miles away and yet they are crystal clear to me …

Feeling confused I blink my eyes and look again. Crystal clear.

I look more closely at the people and shops I am passing. Crystal clear. I look ahead to the convention center, further down the street. Crystal clear.

What?

I've had bad eyesight all my life. Wearing an eye patch as a toddler, graduating to glasses and thank-the-heavens contact lenses at sixteen years old, my poor eyesight has always been something I have struggled with. *Bane of my existence* might be dramatic, but close.

This is a miracle!

I can see!

"Oh, my goodness, how is this possible that I can suddenly see everything crystal clear...?" I quietly exclaim. "My eyesight has miraculously been cured!"

It's the only plausible explanation that I can come up with. My eyesight, after fifty-five years, has been cured. I'm grateful, overwhelmed, and excited at the same time! Wow! It must be because I am at this monumental event.

What should I do?

I call my family and tell them. Call after call, I cry and say that my eyesight has been miraculously cured! My family is not sure what to think, but they are excited for me. After about an hour, I am emotionally spent and decide I need more time to process. I will attend the day's events, but I'll keep my miracle to myself.

The Parliament is more incredible than I imagined, with people of all faith and spiritual traditions intermingling in conversation and wisdom sessions. Looking around, I feel special, not only to be a part of this great gathering—but because I believed that my eyesight being cured during the Parliament was a sign that I had been chosen because I have great work to do.

Around midday, I can no longer keep my miracle to myself. Sitting on a multi-colored pillow in the beautiful Red Tent space, amidst many open and welcoming women, I spill my story. The women are thoughtful and encouraging, and their response gives me the confidence to share more.

And share I did! I almost shouted my miracle from the rooftops, telling everyone I met! Everyone was kind, encouraging, and some even impressed.

It was confirmed. I was special. I was chosen. I had great work to do.

Everything was heightened. My experience of the day was more enjoyable than other days. My joy at feeling special was a new experience for me. I was fully present in every moment, valuing every interaction. I paid close attention because I knew I was to do great things… and I was grateful to be chosen.

Lying in bed that night, I kept pinching myself, marveling at my good fortune. Since an unexpected divorce about five years earlier, I had been searching to find meaning in my life. Jumping into the spiritual waters with both feet, I'd had many heart-opening experiences, but still I searched. I felt there was more. I wanted more… to be more, to do more. And now it had happened.

A new day dawns.

After sleeping fitfully, I jump out of bed before my alarm, excited to meet one of my seminary sisters for an early morning session. Grabbing some clothes, I dash into the bathroom, trying to be as quiet as possible. I ignore the irritation in my eyes, deciding it's from my lack of sleep. *A quick shower and some makeup and I will be on my way,* I think—happy not to have to worry about "putting in my eyes" as I used to call my contact lenses.

The irritation worsens, and so does the sinking feeling in my stomach. "It's not possible," I keep telling myself. "I'm just tired."

A feeling of dread comes over me until I can't ignore it any longer. I have felt this eye irritation before, many times, when my contact lenses were in too long and my eyes had become dry.

No, no, no. It's not happening.

But I must check. Summoning all my courage, I take a deep breath, say a prayer asking it not to be true... and pull on the corner of my eye.

Pop! Out comes a contact lens.

I sink to the floor in disbelief, tears streaming from my eyes. "No! This isn't happening."

"I'm not special! My eyesight wasn't miraculously cured!" I berate myself, realizing I was so tired the first night I got to Salt Lake City, I forgot to take my contact lenses out.

My confidence and sense of self are shattered. "Why is this happening? What about me?" I moan. "Why aren't I special?"

Enough About Me.

Leaning on the sink, muffling my cries so they won't wake my roommate, I vacillate between feeling distraught that I am really *not* special and humiliated that not only did I believe I was... I'd told everyone I met I was. *What a fool I am!*

Knowing I'd be further humiliated if my roommate found me in a crying heap, I decide to pull myself together, get dressed, and get out of there.

I grab the new cardigan sweater purchased especially for this trip and turn it around to slip my arm through the sleeve. The label catches my eye.

No way. This is crazy! Almost crazier than me believing my eyesight had been cured. But there it is… in plain sight.

Enough About Me is the label on my sweater.

I begin to cry again, this time in wonder and gratitude for the unseen, yet ever-present, support we all have. I know in that instant—staring at the words Enough About Me—that I have a very real choice. I can stay in my small, personal focus of finding meaning in my life and making it all about me… my experiences, my feelings, my spiritual expansion… me, me, me… or I can choose to expand my focus… to the We.

Yes, I decide. *Enough about me.*

We are all special. Time for the We.

Misfit to Mystic
by Rev. Dr. Temple Hayes

United, we stand; divided, we are merely a distraction.

As a teenager, the realization that I was drawn more to women than to men caused a division within me. The church said I was going to hell. My grandmother mourned that she would not see me in heaven.

At fourteen years old, I was too young for a driving permit, and my grandmother was telling me—her former-favorite-granddaughter—that she would not see me in paradise. That day, a part of me died a little.

I felt divided.

We had so many untold secrets. Some of those secrets kept us up at night.

When I was ten years old, my mother was accused of having an affair. We lived in a small southern town, and to this day, I still do not know if it was the truth or an accusation. What is true is that it was the sixties in the South. Our life was just like the one they featured in the famous film

Prince of Tides. We swept unacceptable things under the rug and did not look back. We did not talk about anything that made us uncomfortable. We medicated before we meditated.

After this accusation of adultery happened, my family sent my mom to a mental hospital and me up North, to be with more distant family. She was gone for a long time, and when she returned, she had very little of her memory in place. Her body had also been affected by the hospital's therapeutic methods for treatment.

They used barbaric shock treatments on her. My mom was never the same again.

We never spoke of these events. I certainly tried to, but no one would engage. Needless to say, at fourteen, when my father walked in on me and my female teenager more-than-a-friend lover, my parents took *me* to the mental health clinic. My father was not going to have a homosexual daughter.

My family forbid me from ever seeing my teenage, more-than-a-friend, first love again. I went from being the family favorite to the one who had whispers around her name. The hurt of abandonment and betrayal was often unbearable.

That day was a defining moment in my life. I refused to be sent away to some hospital and put in a straitjacket.

Metaphorically speaking, a straitjacket *was* placed upon me, and I would wear it unconsciously for many years.

I found a new way to cope. I drank my feelings away and became a full-blown alcoholic for the next fifteen years.

Drawn to the crescent moon and star, at age eighteen, I had a tattoo put on my arm. My aunt, who already believed I was of the devil, shared that it needed to be removed from my arm because it was the Islamic flag. Well, who knew that at the time? Certainly not me.

Years later, I discovered that on the day I was born, the crescent moon and star were shining brightly in the sky. One person's flag is another's future.

To wish upon a star is progress; to know you are a star is evolution. I wrote that to explain that all of us are born with a purpose. As Mark Twain said, "There are two important days in a person's life: the day you were born, and the day you discover why."

The dichotomy for me was, I always felt connected to God—but the God the preacher talked about hated me and would destroy me in eternal hell. That's a lot for a teenager with no safe place to turn and no guidance for processing.

I found Unity when I was nineteen.

It was the first time in my life I heard, "God loves everybody."

How is this possible? I wondered. All my life, I had heard about a God I wanted to love, but who, based on what I was told, was not the God for me.

During this time, my minister realized I volunteered for everything and came to every activity. One night, she invited me to dinner. We were discussing food choices when, out of the blue, I said, "I want you to know I am gay." She continued to talk about food.

So, I said, "Did you not hear me?"

"Yes, but in Unity, being gay does not matter, for God loves and accepts everyone," she calmly answered.

For the first time in my life, I felt like I belonged and probably took my largest breath of life since being born. I felt undivided. Often these emotions are so deep, and the pain is so great, that even as we mature into adults, the underlying emotions make subtle decisions for us. My emotions were subtle influencers that deeply affected me unconsciously.

They were also my straight jacket.

Throughout my early years, I was terrified that people in white uniforms were going to take me away, just as they had taken away my mother. It was so clear; I didn't belong anywhere. I was a misfit.

The longer I lived, the more I realized that, if you have an unresolved need to belong, you will always be weakening your strengths, possibilities, and self-esteem. From my time as a child raised in the sixties until I was more than fifty years old, my "underneath-feeling" would call my name many times.

"Yea, though I walk through the valley of the shadow of death." Isn't that what it states in Scripture? Needing to belong was my shadow.

Then one day, I had the greatest epiphany of my life. In a few moments, my grief evolved into immense laughter. I found my freedom.

As an original and unrepeatable creation of God, I will *never* belong.

"Yippee!" the angels sang. And with their song, I was resurrected and claimed my space, transformed from misfit to mystic. I laughed for an hour, and I have been in joy ever since. My entire life made sense, and for the first time ever, I felt undivided and absolutely clear.

The excellent teachings in David Friedman's book, *The Thought Exchange* supported me in healing old wounds. The author shares how you will often have thoughts of fear or discomfort, but they are only sensations; they are *not you*. I started using this awareness in different situations of my life.

One day on an airplane, a woman seated beside me began a conversation.

"What does your husband do?" she asked.

The *sensation* took over my whole body. I stayed with the feeling but said to her, "I don't have a husband; I have a wife."

No one died when I said it. Most importantly, I didn't die a little by changing the subject, nor did I shut down my heart. I embraced the sensation of freedom.

Each time I share my story, the power and pain of the story is divided by the number with whom I share it. The experience on the plane gave me the courage to move forward and teach the New Members Class, of which I was the Spiritual Leader. I shared my story and spoke my truth to forty-four people about why Unity matters to me, acknowledging how Unity had saved my life.

No one died of shock, and no one quit the church.

People applauded. The next week, on Sunday, I told my story to the community, which consisted of hundreds of people. *Well, that is powerful,* I thought during my heart-share when they gave me three standing ovations. I thought my task at heart-sharing was completed, because I had greatly healed my fear of abandonment or betrayal.

Two weeks later, Lifetime Television called me. I thought, *No way!* Yet, I did it. I shared my stories from my young childhood to adulthood, which freed me from the closet for my lifetime.

Since then, my life has been dedicated to teachings that unite and heal the divisions within us. The lessons are for anyone who has been shamed by religiosity or toxic family systems or beliefs.

In 2013—just as my third book, *When Did You Die?* was published—I called my psychic friend to get insight on the book. My journey from misfit to mystic was complete, as exemplified by a revelation she shared.

"Your grandmother is coming through with a message," she said.

"Oh yeah. That's my mom's mom, Ruby. She comes through all the time as a voice, or sometimes I can just feel her presence," I replied.

"No. This is your father's mother, named Lois. She wants you to know that you were right and that she is very sorry about everything. She says she has learned so much in the afterlife."

The Aha! moment.

The beauty of the self-actualization is, I had already been doing so much work on myself that it was unnecessary for my deceased grandmother to reassure me. Still, it was nice to hear she had an awakening on the "other side." She was the same woman who had grieved and had told me she would not see me in heaven because I would be in hell. It made me happy to know she had let go of her judgment of me. I felt a sense of completeness and love.

It is interesting that the quote under the title of my story first came to me a few years ago. I thought of it relative to organizations, communities, societies, or families. As time went on, I realized this statement is most significant concerning my life experiences as a gay person.

Divided, I am merely a distraction; but United, I stand.

The Magic Tree
by Judy Lemon

We entered the time of No Time where everything is one,
and I became one of them.

Evening is falling in the Amazon jungle. I arise from my hammock to light a candle and pause to listen as the night chorus begins. Thousands of insects sing their beautiful night song all around me as I contemplate what I am about to do.

In a little while, I am going to leave the safety of my wooden hut—called a *tambo*—to engage in a ritual that is part of my shamanic apprenticeship with Luis, a native Peruvian medicine man. It is a ceremony that aspiring apprentices have performed for hundreds, if not thousands, of years.

But I am not a jungle native. I am a White woman from a completely different culture—and right now, I'm wondering if I'll come back out alive.

Tonight, I am going to sit out there alone in those dark woods full of wild animals, drink a hallucinogenic tea, and dance with the spirits.

While the plant spirit medicine, ayahuasca, is now almost an everyday word, I did not suddenly decide I wanted to be a jungle shaman's apprentice and learn how to conduct healing ceremonies. No, the spirit of this master plant teacher, Madre (mother), had to lure me in and seduce me with her incredible magic.

Through a series of very Spirit-driven events some years before, I'd met my first teacher, Javier, who'd peered at me in a curious way. After feeling like I was being read and analyzed, he suddenly stood up straight as he made a decision.

"If you want to be a healer, I can help you, but you must live in the jungle with me. It will not be easy, but you are strong. I can see it."

And so, I did. I returned to Peru and lived in the jungle with him and other beautiful indigenous people for several months, having a great many adventures as I acquired spirit guides and immersed myself in a culture that was a world away from my own.

But I was never left alone as I would be tonight.

Two days earlier, as I was finishing my lunch of grilled river fish and yucca root, Luis strolled over to the table.

"I want you to come with me. I am going to show you something. Put on your boots and I'll meet you at your *tambo*."

I'd learned not to ask too many questions as an apprentice. Luis has a temper and no patience for fools. When I dare to ask a question, his eyes grow wide as if I'd committed some transgression and he shakes his head.

"You ask too many questions, Judita! You go back to your *tambo* and ask the spirits!" he'd sputter as he'd turn on his heels to stalk away from me.

Knowing that he didn't like to be kept waiting, I dashed back to my little house and climbed up the ladder, pushed open the trapdoor, and grabbed my knee-high rubber boots. As I pulled them on, I heard Luis outside asking me if I was ready.

"Yes! Right now!"

I practically slid down the ladder and bounced over to my teacher. He looked me up and down with a critical eye and grunted.

"Follow me!"

There was another man with him, Mishin, an indigenous Shipibo who did not wear shoes. Luis often pointed out to me that the soles of Mishin's feet were as thick as leather.

Trudging behind them, I struggled to keep up with their rapid pace. We entered a path that was completely overgrown with plants. Both men cleared the way with their machetes where necessary. Steamy and stumbling, I managed to keep myself upright as rivulets of sweat ran down my body.

Luis stopped at an unusual-looking tree that had many roots. It stood alone in what would have been a small clearing if it hadn't been for all the overgrowth. He gazed up at it tenderly, put his hand on its trunk, and gave it a little pat. Mishin stood off to the side as if he knew what was about to happen.

"This is a *renaco* tree. It is very special."

Looking at him, I nodded and waited for him to continue.

"It is time for you to take the next step in your training. You must face your deepest fears in order to be a strong shaman. I want you to do a solo ceremony at night under this tree. Alone. I will not be here with you."

A hundred scenarios flashed through my mind at once. A jaguar might eat me. A giant anaconda might wrap itself around me and squeeze the life out of my bones. Millions of mosquitos would suck every drop of blood from my veins. What if it rained? Me, alone in the Amazon jungle, at night! I decided my worst fear were swarms of mosquitos and chose my words carefully.

"Yes, Luis, I can do this. Um, I'm kind of wondering if I can do it under a mosquito net though. I could easily hang one from this branch here. If not, I'll get eaten alive! I won't be able to sing without eating them, you know?"

Luis and Mishin exchanged glances, and I'm sure at least one of them rolled his eyes.

"It is not traditional to use a net, Judita. Can you imagine my teacher if I told him I was so afraid of little bugs that I needed to hide under a mosquito net? That would have been the end of everything."

"Yeah, I know. But you are from here and don't suffer as much from the bites like we foreigners do. One bite lasts an entire week and I itch like crazy."

"They will not be so bad after dark, but if you feel like you want to use a net, I suppose it will be okay."

Feeling victorious, we agreed that the foray to my fears would be in two nights.

Patting the tree again, he said, "I have always wanted to do ceremony here in this place, but none of the tourists would ever come here, because they want to stay inside. You will be the first to do this. Mishin will clear this entire area so the snakes will not have anywhere to hide. He will do this tomorrow. Yah, Mishin?"

The other man nodded solemnly, then the two of them patted each other on the back and began talking rapidly about what needed to be done.

I'm sure I heard the word *mosquito net* several times and wondered if they thought I was a wimp.

The following morning, I wandered over to the kitchen area for my usual meal of grilled fish and a starch, this time some potatoes.

"Mishin is already working on your area!" Luis announced proudly.

"Really? How's he going to clear that whole path and area around the tree?"

"With his machete, of course. We do not have your big machines. It will take him all day long to get it ready for you. Probably tomorrow too."

I suddenly felt a lump rise in my throat. One man was going to spend an entire day or more clearing that entire long path and ceremonial space with a hand blade just so I could share their age-old tradition. I decided I had to check this out for myself after I ate.

After pulling on my trusty boots once more, I wandered over to the head of the path to see that Mishin had indeed been hard at work. Now I was able to see the actual trail, which had been cleared on both sides for a few yards. The muscular man was farther down the trail, bent over and whacking away at the dense greenery as if he were the machine. Hearing my approach, he turned and waved briefly, then got back to his task. I walked very slowly back to my *tambo*, feeling the enormity of what these two men were doing for me, a clumsy White woman who was afraid of little bugs.

The work was not completed until the following morning. Luis would not allow me to go check out the spot until he called me.

"Judita! Come! It is time to see what Mishin has done for you!"

Disengaging myself from the heavy cotton hammock, I quickly put on my rubber boots again and joined my teacher. He seemed excited and walked faster than ever.

This time, we did not have to whack greenery out of the way. The path to the tree was open and clean, and soon, we were standing in what was now a true clearing. Mishin stood there, still holding his machete, sweat running down his face and dripping onto his bare torso.

I looked around in awe at the work he'd done over the past two days. For me. He had done all of this for me. I felt my eyes tear up and looked at Luis, and in that moment, I decided.

"What do you think, Judita? Do you still want to do the ceremony here?"

"Yes, Luis. And I will not use the net. I want to do the ceremony the way you did it, the way the ancestors did it. I am no longer worried about mosquitos."

Somewhere deep down, I heard a click, as if something had been finalized.

We all headed back down the path to the camp, and I returned to my *tambo*. Yes, these two men did all this for me. I was not going to be a wimp and disappoint them.

Earlier in the day, I had taken a few items to the clearing. I needed a chair to sit in and a small table to use as an altar. Emerging from one of these errands, I ran into Luis, who was checking on my preparations.

"You will begin at seven o'clock and we will go for three hours. I will be energetically watching over you from the maloca. You can go as long as you want, but I will go to bed at ten."

I nodded. I would let Madre and the spirits decide how long the ceremony would be.

"Well, if I'm going to face swarms of mosquitos, I'm going to make it difficult for them," I determined. I put on several layers of clothes, topping off the outermost layer with a hooded rain poncho. Snapping on my headlamp, I made my way slowly to the sacred *renaco* tree and looked around mortified.

I greeted the spirits of the jungle.

"Well, here we are. Just me and you guys out there."

Looking up, I was relieved to see the sky was clear. You never know what the weather will be like in the tropics. One minute it can be dry, and a short time later, you're in a deluge and trudging through rivers of mud.

I began the space clearing and ceremonial preparation, and then sat down in the white plastic chair. I'd drank ayahuasca many times before, but never outside on my own like this. After blessing the brew, I poured myself a cup and drank slowly. I picked up my leaf rattle, the *shacapa*, and began to sing my *icaros*, the sacred songs that drive the ceremony. They protect the space and the participants and direct the spirits to whatever needs to be done.

As the medicine took hold, a beautiful light seemed to fill the clearing. I was seated under the precious renaco tree, feeling it tower over me like a protector. The visions came in slowly, and I looked up through the branches and saw the stars glimmering in the Amazon sky. It was the most beautiful thing I had ever seen! The jungle was alive, and I was a part of it!

And the mosquitos? Oh yes, they were also there. I sang with the leaf rattle in front of my face and swished it back and forth like a windshield wiper. Sure, I ate a few of them, but nothing ate *me*. As I sang, I could hear various animals crunching through the underbrush, and every now and then I'd see a pair of eyes peering at me, but nothing entered my space.

I could feel the spiritual connection with my teacher across the camp, and with the spirits of the ancestors who danced with me. We entered the Time of No Time where everything is one, and I became one of them.

I had faced my fears and received a prize beyond imagining. This would be a night I would never forget.

The next morning, Luis and I exchanged a smile, a knowing.

"You are going to be a good healer, Judita. I'm proud of you!"

I was pretty proud of me, too!

Change of Heart
by Mike Pitocco

We learned the power of salvation.

She was perfect. Beautiful. Those eyes, that smile.

How could I have rejected her? What kind of person did that make me?

Now, a second chance.... unbelievable. And undeserved. Thankful didn't begin to express my feelings. A gracious God had responded to my rejection by giving me another chance to accept His gift of life.

I still had a lot of rough edges at the time. I didn't quite know how to go about expressing the love that welled up inside of me. In many ways, I was new at this love thing. God would use her to continue His work on my heart.

Let me start at the beginning. I had left home, years earlier, emotionally handicapped, incapable of providing the care and nurturing that healthy relationships require. The realization of my inability to do so turned me into an angry, frustrated person. My wife Sharron and stepson Sean had been through a great deal...victims of my immaturity. Sarcasm and silence were weapons I wielded with deadly effect. I hid behind cutting, hurtful remarks rather than dealing with the source of my discontent.

Emotional growth is a process, not an event.

Marriage was my first serious relationship, and it exposed who I was. Every part of me wanted to be a different person: warm, loving, caring, supportive... all the things Sharron and Sean deserved. I desperately desired to change.

Sharron was all the things I wanted and needed to be. She had been raised in a warm, loving home and carried that spirit into our home. She had an amazing inner strength I admired. We would separate three times over the next several years... each time, inexplicably, reuniting. Something beyond us kept pulling us back together.

It was during one of our separations that Sharron told me she was pregnant. My response was to convince her that ending the pregnancy was the answer. Abortion.

There is no doubt in my mind that Sharron would have gladly accepted this precious gift of life had I shown even a modicum of joy, a hint of support. Sadly, by then I had emotionally beaten her down to the point where she agreed that bringing another life into the chaos of our marriage wasn't an option. I rejected a blessing from God, not for the first time, though the depth of my depravity and lack of compassion were nowhere more evident than here.

Who was this man in the mirror?

I used to like who I was, but that somehow got lost along the way. If this was Mike, I wanted no part of him! I would not have wanted to be friends with someone like me. Unhappy, selfish, unloving. It felt as though I was on a highway with no off ramp, no destination, just going through the motions of an unhappy existence.

We can live with a lot of challenging things in life, a lot of pain, a lot of struggles, but we've got to have hope. Hope provides the light at the end of the tunnel. I was losing hope.

Time passed. Years later, things had improved somewhat. I had a good job. Sharon, Sean, and I had just moved into a new home on an acre of land. As I took a morning walk along a country road, I began to ponder a few of the "big" questions of life. I found myself wondering about my purpose and the meaning of life. Was life more than accumulating possessions, taking vacations, raising a family, working a job, and living for retirement? Sure, those were all good things—but is that all there is?

Those questions ultimately led Sharron and I to a meeting with a local pastor one evening. What would happen next would change my world as I knew it.

The pastor shared some Bible verses that ignited our faith. We both believed there was a God, but we didn't realize that a personal relationship with His Son, Jesus Christ, was possible. We learned the power of salvation and that evening—December 2, 1980—by faith, we invited Jesus into our hearts.

There was no burning bush, no fire from above.

But slowly, over time, with prayer, Bible study, sound teaching and preaching, and rubbing shoulders with mature believers, God began to break through my pride, anger, and control. You might say He did a major reconstruction of my heart, a spiritual heart transplant. I began to learn the meaning of surrendering to His will for my life. He let me know

I needed to make things right at home. My wife and children needed to be my top priority.

My previous depravity did not compare to the height, depth, and breadth of God's love with the birth of our daughter, Christina. God restored to Sharron and I the gift of life we had rejected years prior. A second chance. She was perfect. Beautiful. Those eyes, that smile. We are so thankful! We were blessed with Christina in March of 1983, and with our son Daniel two years later. He is an awesome, merciful, loving God.

God didn't force His way in.

God showed me over time the importance of growing in love toward Him, my family, and others. I finally opened the door, and God continues to answer my prayers. The Bible says that God will remove our heart of stone and replace it with a heart of flesh (Ezekiel 36:26). That Scripture came alive for me. It will be a work in progress for the rest of my life.

I now react differently in situations where, in times past, I would have responded with hurtful comments or sarcasm… and it feels great! I like who I am becoming… the new creation the Bible talks about. Small victories have become more and more common.

Today I am blessed to have close relationships with Sean, Christina, and Daniel. I am thankful for their forgiveness and their good hearts. They are awesome! I have a better marriage than I ever thought possible, and God continues to use Sharron as a major force in shaping me into the person He wants me to become.

God has shown me that there is absolutely no one beyond His redemptive, transforming power. I am now filled with hope for today and for eternity.

Some Gifts Are Wrapped in Adversity
by Dominique Brightmon, DTM

Growth is happiness.

Imagine yourself opening a gift box, and instead of getting something shiny, you receive a nice, swift kick to the gut.

In 2012, when people thought the world was going to end, I was turning twenty-one and a couple of semesters away from getting my degree in Information Technology (IT). It was going to be a big year for me, but I didn't yet know how big.

One Saturday, my father decided to go for a drive.

A few hours passed. Sometimes Dad would visit his brother "Reds," and while together, they would lose track of time. We assumed he would be home later. We went to sleep that night and awoke the following morning to discover that Dad was still not home.

My mother was worried and called his cell phone. There was no answer. We decided to stay home instead of going to church, as we usually would, and wait for him to return. We called his cell phone multiple times over the next few hours, but still no answer. Finally, we called our Uncle Reds. He said that he didn't know where my father was either. After the conversation ended, we decided to look for my dad. The wild grey goose chase began!

My brother Wayne and I rode around town in my car, looking for Dad in his usual spots, but we did not find him or his charcoal grey Chevy truck. Twenty-four hours had passed since my dad left. It was time to call the police for help.

When the cops arrived, they took our information and put out a silver alert for my dad, because he was eighty-five years old. After they left, we watched TV to take our minds off the stressful situation.

A few hours later, Mom went to bed, and my brother continued to watch more TV. I went into the basement to play video games to escape mentally, and it was certainly an escape. The next thing I knew, it was 1:30 am!

I got on my knees and prayed for my father's safety and discovery.

Immediately, the phone rang. It was a police officer telling us that they found my father in Silver Spring, MD, more than thirty miles away from our house. I picked up the other receiver to listen in on the conversation. They told us my dad was driving on the wrong side of the road and that they had admitted him to a local hospital. After writing down the address and finding the directions on Google maps, we headed to Silver Spring.

We arrived at the hospital and were informed that my father had been diagnosed with Alzheimer's. Looking back, we realized there had been small signs of him having memory loss here and there, but this incident was the most disturbing sign of all. He was no longer allowed to drive after that.

Since my mom was already seeing multiple doctors, this left me to pick up the slack. But we were happy to be reunited, and over time, we adjusted to this new normal. Some days were easier than others.

As the weeks passed, a new crappy moment was waiting to happen.

On the morning of my twenty-first birthday, I awoke disappointed because it was a damp, dreary morning rather than a sunny day. I had classes that morning and evening and decided to attend them, delaying celebratory gratification and instead being a good student. As fate would have it, my attempt at being a good student was postponed due to an incoming gift that wasn't wrapped in paper.

After leaving my house and driving to get gas, the road was a little damp, but it was nothing out of the ordinary. I filled the tank, bought a cup of coffee and a doughnut, and headed off to class. Coming to the first light, I made a left turn, but while in the turn my car slid into the curb and crashed. I was momentarily shell-shocked before realizing I was still alive and time hadn't stopped.

Uninjured, I made a couple of phone calls—first to AAA, to have the car towed, and then to my parents.

Mom answered the phone in her usual upbeat tone, but when she heard what had happened, she said, "What? You got in an accident?"

I reassured her that I was fine, but she panicked and said she was on her way. I'd told her my location.

As the minutes passed, the traffic began building up and causing a jam. A lady knocked on my window to ask if I was alright. When I realized the traffic was piling up because my car was blocking the road,

I frantically told her what had happened. She offered to have a colleague of hers at the Gas & Electric Company next door tow my car off of the street to open the road.

It seemed like a good idea. AAA was nowhere in sight, and towing my car off the road would fix the traffic problem for others.

Just as the truck was coming to tow my car, a police officer appeared and asked what was happening. While driving past me, he'd noticed the traffic jam and immediately backed up his cruiser to investigate the problem.

There I sat in my car with people knocking on my window.

We explained the situation to the officer, and he decided to call a tow truck that was only three minutes away. He didn't want the folks from Gas & Electric to have to be bothered with the situation, even though they seemed happy to help.

The lady who came to my aid asked me again if I was okay. I told her, "Thanks, and yes." She and her colleagues went back to their jobs.

My parents arrived shortly afterward and embraced me. Then my car was towed by the police officer's tow truck, because the AAA truck I'd called wasn't equipped to transport my wrecked car. Thank God Mom still knows how to drive.

We arrived home, and my anxious brother opened the door for us. I immediately noticed his shoe was loose and untied, which warmed my heart because it showed how much he truly cared about me. It appeared he was rushing to help his brother while not concerned about how he looked or if he tripped on his way to the scene.

A few moments later, my mom said, "You came too far to quit now."

That shook me out of my stupor. What did Mom mean by that statement? Then, she offered to let me use her old '97 Dodge Intrepid to get to my first Network Security class. I was a bit hesitant about getting behind the wheel again so soon after my accident, but had no problems driving.

After arriving home from class that night, exhausted from a full day of car worry and classwork, my family had an ice cream cake waiting for me on the dinner table. They sang happy birthday to me. Mom was proud of me for still going to class, despite the day's distractions. I told them all that I loved them. We all embraced and were grateful once again.

"God has big plans for you," Mom said.

Weeks passed, and it was now Autumn with falling leaves of changing colors, temperatures dropping, and classes fully in session. While being a fulltime student, I also had a part-time job at the public library and a new role as an assistant caregiver for my father. All of my learning and jobs filtered into my work.

One day, my boss called me into his office for a meeting because of some complaints made about me by a higher-ranking staff member. My boss told me that some new hires were coming in soon, and I "needed to shape up" because they would look to me as a senior leader. A few days later, during an evening shift, I saw a blue, black, and gold book titled *The 5 Levels of Leadership: Proven Steps to Maximize Your Potential* by John C. Maxwell. After finding out it was also on audio, I grabbed the audiobook, too.

After picking up that book, I became a voracious reader and personal development junkie who created a rock-solid, positive mental attitude. The books helped me solve problems of low self-confidence, poor communication skills, and a lack of emotional intelligence. By acting on the advice from every book, I changed and found a new level of happiness. Getting progressively better at something, big or small, creates happiness. Growth is happiness.

People ask me why I am so cheerful all the time.

I tell them, "I'm a human who still has bad days, but by doing the following four things, I have the happiness most seek. Read good books, listen to something that will benefit you, watch something that will educate or inspire you, and encourage somebody else while keeping yourself encouraged."

My father was ill for five years before he died from Alzheimer's. Reading about being a better caregiver helped me find solace in getting to know him more during that time. Listening to the words of people like Zig Ziglar, John Maxwell, and Brian Tracy helped me become a passionate and promoted professional at work.

An inspirational millennial author who spoke at a Toastmasters meeting inspired me to write books of my own. My mother's encouragement on my twenty-first birthday, after the car crash, always reminded me of my goal to finish my degree.

Although my 2012 year felt like a crappy year, reflecting on it makes me feel happy. The adversity I experienced that year taught me the power of relationships, reading, and reaching for more.

My goal every year now is to read at least fifty books, because books are a gift that can solve problems and create happiness.

Become the Soul's Calling

by Jess Campmans

We can only deny the path of our soul for so long.

"Mystical Warrior—a powerful, graceful, majestic black horse."
I shrank back in my chair, half-intrigued and half-mortified
by my answer to the question, "If you were a horse, what
would your name be?"

After driving over 900 miles to reach this supposedly life-transforming
gathering of horses healing humans, I felt like I had just given up one of
my deepest, darkest secrets.

What if these people laughed and made fun of my horse-name answer?
What if they connected the dots and found out how weird I was? I shifted
uncomfortably in my seat, a chair that now felt hard and unyielding.

My horse name had given me chills as soon as I'd said it out loud.
Yet no one seemed to notice my embarrassment as the facilitator moved
on, encouraging the rest of the people sitting in our circle to offer us a
glimpse into their personal, inner world.

Sitting there listening to the others, I felt like a clue had been revealed to me, a clue that would lead me to a treasure map that had never existed before.

Mystical Warrior, my inner self's horse-name.

At first, it seemed kind of silly to me that all of us in the circle were getting so giddy and lit up over a pretend horse name; it felt more like a child's game than a way to bring healing. But as I watched in awe, the horses began moving freely around the circle of us humans, working collectively and connecting to each person individually. It was as if they were anointing every human with their newfound horse-name and giving us each a chance to feel deeply into what our name meant, uncovering the significance of it within their presence.

My tears began freely falling onto my hands, which were clasped tightly in my lap. Normally, I would have never let myself be caught crying in front of other people—but for some reason, this felt different. Amongst this circle of humans and horses, I felt held by an invisible and unexplainable force. I had no idea why I was crying, but there was no stopping the floodgate of emotion that had sprung from somewhere inside of me.

As my hands reached out to touch the horse nearest me, I couldn't hold on anymore. With a rush, it all came flooding out.

Every day revealed more of my personal treasure map.

The last day of the weekend brought a significant piece to my treasure map when I found myself standing face-to-face with one of the most soul-beautiful women I have ever met. She called herself a *shaman*. The word itself ignited something deep within me.

She carried herself just like the horses: majestic, proud, and full of integrity. Finding the courage to seek her out after our closing ceremony, I asked her what was needed to do to become more like her. Her intense-yet-compassionate gaze struck a chord in me, a place in my soul that felt like it hadn't been touched in years.

"I see a wall around your heart," she said, smiling and softening her gaze as she continued. "It is a very strong wall that needs to be cracked open. You don't need to be like me. You need to work on breaking that wall down to find what it is that you're protecting in there. I promise that what you will find is all that you need to help you become *you*."

And with that she turned and walked away, leaving me in awe and confusion. I had so many questions, but knew she had already given me the answer.

I decided to follow the guidance of my heart.

My drive should have only taken me two days to return home. Instead, filled with a newfound vitality, it took three. I didn't want the buzz of this adventure to end!

Zigzagging back and forth in a northwest direction, each mile allowed me to become more fully immersed in reflection of all that had happened over the weekend workshop. My mind could hardly comprehend everything I was feeling. It was as if the dial of my body's life force had been cranked to high, having witnessed countless miracles.

Driving through the middle of a vast wasteland of scrub and sage, with the only sign of civilization being a ranch gate entryway with a rope dangling like a hangman's noose, I had the distinct sensation of something new happening, something I had never felt before. This sensation persisted and strengthened with each mile I drove.

At first, I resisted it, not understanding what was happening to me. Resistance seemed futile, and as the sensation continued to get stronger, I eventually surrendered to it. My jaw slackened and dropped open of its own accord. In a voice not mine, slowly and haltingly emerged the words: "Thhhaaaank yoouu."

As I listened to myself, I knew these words were not mine.

Simultaneously, I felt the presence of my mother-in-law, who had passed away eleven years earlier. It felt like my jaw wanted to move again, to bring forth more words, but when I tried my best to relax my body and let it happen again—there was nothing.

In the next moment, my entire body went slack and slumped into the seat, as if something had decided that "Thank you" was enough for now. The sensation that had taken up my body as a way to deliver those two words was now gone, leaving me to wonder what had just happened. *Am I going crazy?*

Yet the feeling of gratitude delivered with those two words helped me realize something: I had, somehow, connected to and become a channel for the spirit of my deceased mother-in-law. This was both freaky and fascinating!

Without the full experience of feeling some otherworldly power take over my jaw and move it for me, it is doubtful I would have believed it happened. But there was no denying it.

If this is possible, then what else is possible? I wondered.

The rest of my drive home was spent sinking deeper into the mystery of all that I had experienced, feeling changed but unable to explain how. Excited yet terrified to tell anyone, I kept the story of my other-worldly experiences to myself.

However, despite my reluctance to share, these experiences kept happening. I couldn't conceal my new connection to the spirit world, which had somehow found me. The more I tried to hide or ignore it, the more prevalent it became in my life, creating a rift within me that felt like self-abandonment.

Ultimately, this caused me to reconcile these parts of myself.

With this newfound ability, I tuned into my horse Eagle.

My hope was to better understand the direction and purpose he wanted to bring to my own healing herd of horses, Guided by Equus. Eagle asked me to witness the release of the "war horse/tough one" archetype and the bringing into being a new mastery for the soul of that archetype. He explained their place in our current reality no longer exists. Many horses are misunderstood because of their unique qualities of high sensitivity, which in the past kept their riders from death.

Eagle questioned me how to best serve the world now with these same qualities, and the word *Teacher* dropped into my awareness. He offered to release from the Horse Consciousness the outdated archetype of War Horse and integrate Wise Teacher in its place.

At this request, I witnessed an army of war horses come to the forefront of my mind. They formed a line and bowed down on one knee in recognition of this.

As my awareness jolted back to my current reality and the solid chestnut horse in front of me, silent tears streamed down my face.

Once again, I had to ask myself what had just really happened ... the communication, the vision, the feeling of being part of something very profound.

We can only deny the path of our soul for so long.

Suddenly, as if by magic, what becomes possible is more powerful than anything we could have dreamed. Without knowing why, one day I found myself leaning against the warm body of one of my horses, feeling soul-level exhausted.

"I'm so tired of being here and doing this," I sobbed. "I just want to go home!"

The words had slipped out of my mouth almost unconsciously. "I just want to go *home?*"

From deep within, an intense feeling washed over me. Leaning against the side of my horse, I felt safer, more alive, and more at home than ever before. Slowly, it began making sense to me. Saying those words meant this human body, this existence, here on this Earth plane— was not all there was to life.

My sigh of relief released the tears caught in my throat. My body relaxed into the comfort of the solid fur body beside me, home to the spirit of a soul companion. Everything that hadn't made sense in the moments before, now did from this new perspective.

Discovering the path of my soul that began by connecting to a pretend horse-name helped me find the mystical warrior within me. My fear of being "found out" gave way to something even greater: finding my greatest insights, inspirations, and joys through my connection to spirit.

My fear of being judged challenged me to discover my joy. Instead of being *weird,* I was actually *wired*—wired as a channel of spirit.

I now understand life through my sacred relationship to the wisdom of my soul. I listen more deeply, open myself up, take risks, and feel inspired and empowered … as I revolutionize my life to become my soul's calling.

Home Is Where the Heart Is
by Teresa Velardi

My word for 2020 is Release.

"Yes, we can help you! We will modify your loan," the seemingly helpful customer service representative at the bank said. "Just print and fill out the pages you'll see on our website for modification. Remember, you must be three months late in your mortgage payments to qualify, so don't send us any money. When the ninety days pass, send us the application and supporting documentation, and we will modify your loan."

I felt both relief and annoyance when I heard those words.

Unfortunately, I had just made a house payment before calling the bank. Due to an injury, I wasn't working, and my partial disability income was about to end. There hadn't been enough money in my account to pay the mortgage, so I had cashed some savings bonds and sold my jewelry to make the payment.

If I had known *not* to make a mortgage payment, I would have already been thirty days into the process. Oh well, at least there was one solution coming as I awaited the approval for full disability. Or so I thought …

"Okay, I'll go to your website and do that, thank you!"

Those were the last words I said to the woman from the bank, who assured me my home loan would be modified. I felt surrounded by angels and covered in Heaven's grace. Everything would be okay. *My house will still be my home,* I wrote in my journal.

At the end of the ninety days, just as I prepared to confirm the mailing address, the doorbell rang. A FedEx guy handed me an envelope from the bank. I thought for sure it contained instructions and a return envelope for my documents to get the modification going. But I got the surprise of my life.

Notice of intent to accelerate! Foreclosure?

This must be a mistake!

I immediately called the bank and was told, "Disregard the documents delivered by FedEx, because the bank is in the process of modifying the loan."

The woman confirmed the address, and I sent off the correct documents to the loan modification department.

Every week brought a new foreclosure notice delivered to me by FedEx. And every call to the bank brought the same response: "Pay no attention to the foreclosure documents. We have your documents, but we need something else."

This process continued until a notice of default from the court came in one of those FedEx envelopes. *What*? The foreclosure train was speeding down the tracks! In court, the judge gave me time to address the matter. In the meantime, the modification department was losing pages of paperwork I had repeatedly sent to them. The documents arriving at my door, some relating to modification, and some to foreclosure, had my head spinning.

As a single woman with no legal education, I needed help.

A friend suggested a man named Charlie who could possibly assist me with this mess. Charlie offered some support in preparing legal documents and promised he had a program that would hand me my house back, supposedly free and clear of *any* mortgage.

Although a house clear of debt would be a huge bonus, my main concern was getting some help with the modification paperwork and process—but $3,500 later, the mortgage was still not modified, and the bank seemed even more intent to foreclose.

Until now, I had been my own attorney. Charlie introduced me to an attorney named Frank, who agreed to go to court with me. Of course, Frank required payment upfront—and after his one court appearance on my behalf, Frank died. He had cancer that was further along than he knew. It was sad, and I was on my own again.

Let me back up a minute to the day the FBI rang my doorbell.

I was at a conference in California when my son called to tell me FBI agents were at my house.

"For what?"

Then I remembered that my helper, Charlie, had said, "The FBI will be notified of the situation with the bank, because the bank is perpetrating a fraud."

I talked to the agent and made an appointment for after my return. At the office of the FBI, I was astonished to find out they were investigating *Charlie*. OMG!

After the agents grilled me about the situation with my house, they moved on to another form of intimidation.

Agent Jerry, who did most of the talking, tried his best to convince me to wear a wire into the courtroom when both Charlie and my attorney Frank would be present. The FBI wanted to hear every word.

"You're kidding, right?" I said.

"No," he replied. "You'll just come to the office before you go to the court. We'll tape the wire on you, test it, and we'll be able to hear the entire conversation."

"But what about the metal detector I have to go through before getting into the court? The detector will pick it up for sure!" I said.

He shrugged.

"You're asking me to put my integrity and freedom on the line."

I wasn't about to risk this for anyone, not even an FBI agent. He was ticked-off because I refused to play his game.

However, I did say, "I could record whatever transpires on my smartphone tucked inside my bra. I'm not sure how much you will hear, but I'd rather do that than risk wearing a wire."

As if the mess with my home was not enough, now it seemed the FBI was after *me*.

When we met later, Agent Jerry said turning over the recording would nullify my attorney-client privilege with Frank. I felt like the one under investigation.

Trusting my gut, I decided not to turn the recording over to the FBI agents. Agent Jerry's response was, "This is the only chance you'll get."

"Seriously? To do what? I'm being victimized by the bank. I was just looking for help to get out of court and into a modified mortgage, and now you're threatening me?" I was livid!

I never heard from the FBI agents again. You can't make this stuff up. It felt like I was playing a part in a big-screen crime drama.

Many trips to court and to gather information followed. I found help on phone calls with groups of people who were going through similar challenges during the 2008 economic crisis. I knew there was something bigger at play. However...

Meaningful coincidences and synchronicities began to appear in my life.

Being the courageous woman God created, I put on my Armor of God to fight the good fight—even when I don't want to.

On the day I headed into federal court, my morning reading and journaling time focused on Scripture about the Armor of God. I also received a daily text message scripture sent to me by a pastor friend. The scripture that came to my phone that day was also about the Armor of God!

Prayerfully, I asked God to send an army of angels into the courtroom with me. Then, I got in my car. On the way to the courthouse, I turned on what I thought was the radio, but instead, it was the CD of Joyce Meyer's teaching on ... you guessed it... the Armor of God!

I'd always felt God's hand in the entire grueling, sometimes heart-wrenching, process of trying to save my house—including the day the judge's gavel granted summary judgment to the bank. The attorney for the bank had lied, but the judge believed him more than me.

Previously, that attorney had told me he knew I was right, but he had to represent the bank to "feed his family."

My thought was, *Oh, I see. So you sold your soul to the devil.*

I still trusted God would have my back while I wore His armor.

This journey has taken me to every court except the Supreme Court of the United States. There came the point when I knew I would have to leave the house. Unsure of my moving date, I told my son he had to move out and find his own place. He needed to stay in the area for his business, and I did not want him impacted by my problems or left without a roof over his head. Losing your home affects the whole family.

When he asked me where I would go, I said, "I don't know. Maybe I'll pack it all up, put it in storage, and go for a ride!"

"You can't do that, Mom! You're too old," he said.

I asked him what rule book he was living by, and we both had a good laugh. He knows me.

Ten years later, after many visits to the courtroom, I'm still in my house.

Finally, I was given a move-out date and hired a company to conduct an estate sale. My pottery studio was transferred to the home of a good friend who has been making pottery with me for nearly eighteen years. I then prayed for direction.

I had previously packed up what I would keep and put it in storage. My furniture—except for my bed, a dresser, my desk, some shelves, and a buffet table—was all sold.

When people ask, "Where are you going?" I shrug my shoulders. The truth is, how long I will be able to stay is unknown. That decision seems to change daily.

It's also a mystery whether the bank will say, "Let's just give her the house," or what will happen next. This year has been full of many surprises, and I haven't yet decided who of my many friends I want to visit first! But one of the things that will undoubtedly be packed to go with me is the Armor of God. I wear it every day.

At the beginning of each year, I choose a word. My word for 2020 is Release. After being verbally dragged through the mud by so many people in the legal field, it was time to fully surrender, release this situation to God, and let Him show me what's next. "Let go and let God" became my mantra.

One thing I know for sure is this: When I decided to release control over the things that were binding me, I received so much more peace, joy, and time to do what fills me up—more blessings than I could have imagined.

So, you might ask, what keeps me going and makes me most happy? Even though I may someday be without a house, I always have a home in the heart of God!

Mercy
by Dr. Anne Worth

The lock was open. The love of God was the key.

I couldn't remember a time when I had been more apprehensive. What strange force had overtaken my brain and volunteered me to stand before the fire-breathing God of my youth? *Come on, I told myself, you're over-reacting. You can do this.*

Walking toward the ballroom of a local hotel, I wondered if I might stress myself into a heart attack. With each step, my heart pounded faster and harder inside my chest.

Why was I so afraid? There was no physical danger here, but ridicule and condemnation can hurt even more than being hit. What will those God-believers think of me? How will they treat me?

I was no stranger to condemnation. *I can handle whatever those people think of me. But what is God going to think?*

Entering the cavernous room, we were told to sit in the interlocking, straight-back chairs and be quiet. The leaders were abrupt. They certainly intended to control the other sixty-five people and me sitting obediently in silence.

Everyone else seemed calm, but I felt like a sheep being led to slaughter.

The hefty double-doors closed. Were they locked? I surprised myself by muttering, "God, I'm sorry." I didn't realize those words were a prayer of repentance. Tears began running down my cheeks before a word was said.

A long line of workshop leaders introduced themselves as they stood at the front of the room and warned that we would get out of the workshop only what we put into it. Suddenly, everything went totally black, and Gloria Estefan's voice filled the room.

She sang about a woman who had searched every moment of her difficult life to believe something would "bring her out of the dark." Love saved her and brought her into the light. She knew she would make it. I related to every word of the song... except being in the light.

Will I ever make it out of the darkness?

While contemplating that idea, a bright light flooded the room. Almost everyone was crying. I knew where my tears were coming from, but why were all these Christians crying?

The long week had officially begun.

For the first few days, we heard lectures that were psychological and philosophical. It was nothing new to me, and my impatience grew. During almost every session, they played some tear-jerking song, obviously trying to tug at my emotions.

Days stretched far into the night, and slowly but surely, the process brought me closer to my family history and my experiences with God.

The leaders were kind and caring, tenderly helping me face the betrayal and abuse from my family and the condemnation from the church. They were sad that caregivers, who should have treasured me, had instead convinced me I was unlovable. They criticized any church experiences that made children believe they were sinful and unforgivable. Those false beliefs had almost been too much for me to bear.

Not one person in the group condemned me.

"You're not bad, you're just a human being," they said. "Without God's help, life is too difficult for any of us to live well."

Who was this helpful God of which they spoke? I didn't know a helpful God. Now I was face-to-face with the questions that had brought me into this room. But the session was over. There was no opportunity to ask my questions or reiterate my beliefs about the absent, judgmental God I knew.

It was the lunch hour, but being so troubled, I couldn't eat a bite.

When we returned to the room, I needed to talk. The lights went out almost immediately. A song was about to change everything.

The words to this song portrayed God as a father singing to one of his children. *God sings?* I tried to imagine anyone singing the words of the song to me. It went like this: God told his child, "I was there when you took your first breath. Though you couldn't see me, any time you cried, my arms were open wide."

Rage started to simmer in my gut. His arms had *never* been "open wide" to me. The more the song continued, the more I seethed. The lyrics crooned that God heard my first prayer and knew every promise I ever made. Then I wept, remembering the dark, lonely nights, trembling and pleading with God to forgive me for all my badness—the distraught nights of anguish when I promised to be good.

But my promises were never kept. I was the bad girl who couldn't be good, no matter how hard she tried. I had felt filthy dirty, and down deep, was still that forsaken, woeful child.

The song finished by saying God would always see me as his child, and that he would pick me up and hold me close.

My voice erupted like a volcano in that quiet room. "No! No! No!" It isn't true!

A flood of profane adult words followed my initial outburst. I was speaking for the little girl who never knew God loved her. Obviously, He was selective and chose some children, but not others. If he was such a good Father and loved all his children, why the hell hadn't he chosen to take care of me?

Why had he let my father and mother abuse me?
Why had he let the church judge me?
Why would he leave me feeling so alone I wanted to die?
He could have prevented it all, and he did nothing!

The group leaders were prepared for my explosion—almost as if they expected it to happen. Instantly, two chairs were set up facing each other. An older man sat in one chair, and I sat in the other.

The man represented God. To every "why" question I hurled at him, he spoke quietly in response.

"I see your pain and confusion," he said. "But you are my child—my beloved child. I have loved you every day of your life. I know it's hard for you to believe my words right now, but today can change everything you believe. If you let me come into your heart, your eyes will be opened, and you will see the truth."

I nearly gagged. Everything he said made me furious.

Pie-in-the-sky clichés weren't going to solve my problems. I didn't trust a syrupy word that came out of his mouth. My protests continued.

So, Mr. God, you're finally going to show up after all these years?
Are you going to heal my broken heart?
Are you going to heal my disease?
Are you going to absolve me from my sins?
Will you let me into Heaven, if such a place even exists?

The man playing God took no offense at anything I said. His expression was sorrowful, but I didn't care. Jesus was a man, and my heart and mind were locked against the silver tongues and sweet words of any and every man. Even if these were the words of Jesus, they didn't penetrate my hard heart. My wall of distrust was thick and strong. I hung on to my unspoken motto:

Never surrender.
Never trust anybody.
Never get your hopes up again.

I'd built a protective wall of distrust around my heart. The thought of believing the words of any man sent a shiver of fear through my body, but I was so tired of fighting my own battles, and tired of fighting this man. Finally having nothing left to say, I sat in silence.

But he still had much to say. He spoke in his quiet, reassuring voice.

"When you admit you need to be saved, when you admit how much you want peace, and how much you wish you had a father, it will open your heart. In all your searching, in all your waiting, you have never found an answer. Let me take your fears. Let me take your sin. You will not be punished for anything you have done, because Jesus paid your debt on the cross. When you accept his sacrifice, you are forgiven, and you can rest in his arms."

His words tugged at my heart. No punishment? Forgiven? Saved? Peace? Good Father? Rest in the arms of Jesus?

Can his promises be true?

He continued, "If you accept Jesus as your savior, he will be waiting for you when your earthly life is over. You will live in Heaven, where you will never shed another tear or know a moment of pain. Your body will be transformed into perfect health. If you believe my words, your uncertainty will be over. I will saturate your heart with everything you have longed for: unconditional, never-ending love, joy, and peace."

I wanted to give in, to totally surrender. The uncertainty was agonizing. My life was at a life-or-death crossroad. He made it sound so easy—just believe.

It wasn't easy.

I slumped over, my face in my hands.

There wasn't a sound in the room except for my weeping. My eyes were closed, but suddenly, in my mind's eye, Jesus stood before me. Everything else disappeared in his majesty.

He was a vision in white, gentle but powerful. His sweet love and cleansing light surrounded me. He knew everything about me and saw me precisely as I was. What did I have that would be of any use to such a being? My sin and shame bent me even lower. Should I fall at his feet?

No, he didn't want that. I imagined that he gently lifted my chin so I could see his face. The kindness and compassion in his eyes held such expanse and depth that all my doubts melted away. Slowly, he extended his hand to me. I saw the nail scars.

When I reached out, the man sitting in the other chair took my hand. I kept my eyes closed and imagined it was the touch of God. It was finished. In every way, God became real.

I didn't want to open my eyes. I didn't want Jesus to go away. But when my eyes did open, His presence still felt very near.

I thought God had been done with me ages ago—but now, nothing about me was so gross that he didn't want to touch me, love me, or heal me. As lost and forsaken as I had been, only the magnitude of God's love expressed in this dramatic imagining could have penetrated my defenses. My life would never be the same.

God alone is worthy of praise, but when he adopted me, I became part of his family even though I didn't deserve it. God changed my name and called me worthy.

God's light drove the lies that had caused me so much pain into the darkness. I had enjoyed fleeting moments of happiness before, and even felt hopeful from time to time, but this was different. I felt the pure love of a good father for His child, a joyful stillness.

The gift Jesus left for me is peace of mind and heart through faith.

I didn't know it yet, but some of the last words Jesus spoke to his disciples were about the peace that keeps our hearts from being troubled. Without

Jesus, I could never have received that kind of profound peace. I'd never known that.

Later that night, I had to laugh at some of my thoughts and shook my head remembering how disheveled and wiped out I looked when meeting Jesus. If asked to describe a conversion scene prior to my experience at Barnabas, I would have pictured an epic Cecil B. DeMille movie.

In the last scene, converts would triumphantly and blissfully walk down the aisle of a magnificent cathedral, maybe wearing white, flowing robes. Tears of joy would stream down their cheeks as they went forward to meet their bridegroom, Jesus. Organ music would fill the sanctuary with a glorious melody and the brilliant light of God would shine through stained glass windows.

But the day I met my Lord, he wasn't looking for a cleaned-up, well-dressed, smiling, Sunday-morning woman. He wanted me, just as I was.

Even after such a supernatural experience—even though every cell of my body knows that Jesus is real—little doubts entered my mind like annoying gnats. *What the heck is this? Where in the hell are these thoughts coming from?*

I still had a lot to learn about living with Jesus while still on the earth. But the lock was open. The love of God was the key. Even though I had not gone willingly, my Father still welcomed me home.

The waiting, the searching, and the hurting was over.

Final Thoughts

Lao Tzu wrote, "A journey of a thousand miles begins with a single step." His words describe the stories in this section. The authors took us on a tour of inner wisdom, trial by fire, and success by love. They dared to bare their souls and shared how the only impossible journey is the one you never begin. All of life—from birth to rebirth as death—is a journey. The journey can be a delayed single trip, as shared by Rev. Ariel Patricia, or a series of life-long adventures, seen in *Misfit to Mystic* by Rev. Dr. Temple Hayes.

Ed Diener, editor of *Perspectives on Psychological Science*,[1] identifies five factors that contribute to happiness in life journeys: social relationships, temperament/adaptation, money, society and culture, and positive thinking styles. The authors in this section traveled through the unknown—but in the end, they embraced the factors listed by Diener, and in the process, found joy.

The stories also pointed out how happiness is affected by cognitive patterns — like seeing opportunities instead of threats and generally trusting and liking other people. Our authors described many of these attributes in their stories.

The stories in this section pointed out that one person's challenge was another person's happiness. Uncertainty can become freedom. The way the journey of life is viewed creates our joy and can turn a situation from crappy to happy.

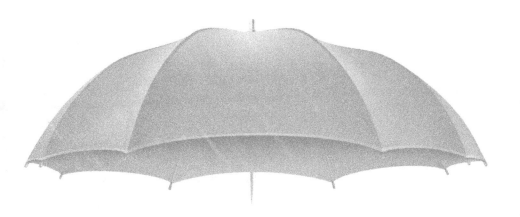

PART 5

WORDS OF WISDOM
If I Knew Then What I Know Now

*We are on a powerful journey
– a sacred journey –
into our shared consciousness*

If given the opportunity for deep reflection, would you have done anything differently in your life? Imagine being able to step into a time machine, travel back in life to meet yourself in your past, and share a few words of insight with yourself. Our authors have done just that for you, and we hope you enjoy their words of wisdom and encouragement.

Dream Journal
Kathleen O'Keefe-Kanavos

If I knew then what I know now, I would have kept a dream journal sooner in life and dreamed more—in order to grieve less. Life and death have taught me that our loved ones are only a dream away. Visiting with me in my dreams is just as important to my deceased loved ones as it is to me. Dreams are sacred doorways to Divine messages from them. And I would embrace my grief rather than try to ignore it, because it is a form of love. Without love, there cannot be grief. Grief is love.

Relax Into the Knowing
Rev. Ariel Patricia

There is a sweetness in life that you can relax into when you take the pressure off yourself. I've learned that you don't have to save the world all by yourself. You don't even have to save it with a few good friends. When you can relax into the knowing that all is ultimately well, joy becomes you.

My Rear-view Mirror
Rev. Dr. Temple Hayes

I would have owned my part to play in this world with joy and excitement rather than feeling cursed and asking God, why me? I would have said each day, "Thank you for the gift of this unique and rebellious me". There would not be one day spent on being invisible yet being magnified. I would know belonging is an asset, but not a necessity, for an original thinker. I would be all I am today, yet sooner. I would be directed by the power of trust, not fear.

Time is Fleeting
Constance Bramer

It's funny how when you are young, you are always looking forward; probably because you don't have much to look back on yet. I didn't know then that time is fleeting, and life has an undetermined timer. Knowing this now, I wish I had treasured more moments with my mom while I had her in my life. I think losing my mother so young has made me hyper-aware of the importance of living "in the moment" and being grateful for the little things in life.

Do More

Bernie Siegel, MD

If I knew then what I know now, I could have done more good for my patients, my family, and the world's residents.

Ooh Child, Things Are Gonna Get Easier

Lorilyn Rizzo Bridges

"Ooh child,

Things are gonna get easier... things'll get brighter ~"

These lyrics could have been my theme song when I was growing up. I spent so much time daydreaming about how I was going to fix my broken world.

Eventually, I gained the wisdom of acceptance.

Life taught me to accept the times when our world feels dark and broken, and trust there'll be times when it'll feel much brighter.

Your struggles will give way to strength; it's the circle of life.

"Some day,

We'll walk in the rays of a beautiful sun... when the world is much brighter ~"

Live in the Moment
Frank Zaccari

My advice to my younger self is to make time and cherish each moment with my family. I was so focused on my career and providing for my family that I was not fully present for many important moments.

Heart IQ
Mike Pitocco

If I knew then…

… that living with eternity in mind helps to put today's problems in proper perspective

… that I didn't have to rely solely on myself to make the changes I so desperately needed to make

… that true joy is found in serving others

… that too much vitamin "I" is bad for anyone

… that love is always worth the risk of a broken heart

… that I was made for a purpose greater than myself

… how to truly love my wife, my children, and others

… the height and depth and breadth of God's love and grace that I know now!

The Key to Success
Judy Lemon

One of the things I've heard repeatedly throughout the years is, "I'll just put it out to the universe!" This New Agey-sounding declaration tends to be uttered enthusiastically by a person who wants to manifest something in their lives. After many years of being disappointed by my own unrealized desires, what I know now is that simply hoping that some nebulous power will hand us our greatest wishes, just for the asking, doesn't work. We must also do our part by making things happen in this physical realm.

Trust What You Know to Be True
Janet Cincotta

If I knew then what I know now, I would have sought an authentic spiritual home for myself sooner. I would have put my trust in what I knew to be true, instead of a faith steeped in hierarchy, self-proclaimed superiority, and contradiction. I would have taken up residence in my heart along a rocky, glacial stream, or on an endless, empty beach, or on a mountaintop overlooking a deep, forested valley. I would have surrounded myself with beauty, embraced solitude, and allowed myself to dream, which is what I think we are meant to do.

The Escape Hatch
Lynn Reilly

During the times in my life I was nearly agoraphobic, hopeless, and feeling perpetually lost, I wish I'd known that vulnerability was a strength and not a weakness, and that every time someone said I was "strong" when I muscled through hardship, it was inviting me to feel, not encouraging me to hold it all in to not burden others. I wish I knew that opening myself up was not only bold and brave, it was liberating. I wish I knew that telling the truth was the escape hatch in the cage I had locked myself in.

Resonance
Tamara Knox

If I knew then what I know now, I would have honored and embodied the universal "hum" that is inside all—attainable and omnipresent. This is the connection to Divine essence and Love, which leads to success and wholeness.

The Gift of Forgiveness
Misty Tyme

I would resolve my anger, pain, and unfilled expectations with my mom much sooner. In turn, my deep and desperate need to be right would not have held such a grip on me. If I had known the real meaning and power of forgiving, I would have given this gift to myself long ago.

Forget Regret
Maria Lehtman

One evening, during a difficult period in my life, I was meditating at home, and I said to the Universe, "This is proving to be almost impossible— what am I to do?" A quiet voice inside me answered, "The only regret is regret itself." I still repeat that sentence in my mind when challenged by a topsy-turvy life. I have lived a rich life and cannot imagine having done things very differently. But through my experience, I grew in patience and felt less regret. If anything, I would have embraced the fact that love is, most of all, patient. Love is all.

Unleash the Goddess Within
Diane Vich

If I knew then what I know now, I wouldn't have let stress constantly take over my life. Obstacles and challenges are an opportunity for us to learn, grow, and evolve. Obstacles can throw us off course, leaving us feeling helpless, hopeless, and alone. A deep connection with yourself stops those negative feelings by creating balanced energy, harmony, and creativity. The hardest step is the first step. Never stop believing in your dream. Don't let others get in your way. You deserve to have the life you dream of. You deserve to unleash the Goddess within and unveil the magic around you.

A Setback is a Story Forward
Dominique Brightmon, DTM

With the knowledge I have now, I would have taken a different route on my way to class and started my personal growth journey sooner. But it feels more rewarding after the accident—because no matter what happens, if you are still alive after that moment, you have someone to teach, inspire, and encourage.

Challenges Grow Us
Jess Campmans

Each of us comes into this life with an opportunity for growth as a soul. Every single person in the world has come up against challenge, because challenge creates opportunity for our soul to grow and evolve. Welcome the unknown, welcome changes, and embrace challenges. Within each of these, we can find the very things we have been searching for in our lives. We grow through the experience of becoming the calling of our soul.

The Journey Through Grief
Deborah J. Beauvais

There may be similarities, but how we journey through grief is different for each of us. Listen to your heart when making decisions and choices. Do what soothes and replenishes you. Take your time. Ask for help. There are no rules. Cry, yell, and let it out. Dis-ease is created by keeping pain inside. Go within, learn who you are, and ask, "What do I need right now?" Honor the need. Nourish your being. If I knew then what I know now, I would have replaced anger with love much sooner.

Our Pets Are Here to Help Us
Ellie Pechet, M.Ed.

I now understand that our pets can come to us as Spirit Guides to help us on physical and emotional levels—or sometimes even to fulfill a sacred contract. I appreciate my cats Snickers and Blue even more deeply knowing this. Agreeing to fit their enormous Spirits into two small cat bodies was their first amazing gift. They stayed with me for twenty-plus years out of love, devotion, and Divine Assignment, and they continue to bless my life now that they are back in the world of Spirit. As we look more deeply at who our pet companions are and why they came to us, we can discover the very rich treasures they are and how they support and guide us.

Trust Your Gut
Catherine Paour

As a young girl, I was envious of kids who could run, and I always felt left behind. As a young adult, I thrived in community service, rather than engaging in physical activities. As a grown woman, I became more aware of my intuition, but didn't realize I'd had it all along. Every surgery I had, plus the birth of my baby, put me at extreme risk—because I didn't know. Today, I often reflect and think back… it would have been really helpful to know that my heart had a giant hole.

Savor the Journey
Helen Heinmiller

If I knew then what I know now, I would have slowed down and enjoyed my small accomplishments more. In my rush to make something grand for myself, I missed the joy of the journey more often than I should have. I cast aside my first "A" in school, my first raise at my job, and my first completed short story before the paint could dry on my internal congratulations banner. Countless accomplishments passed by until I noticed the hourglass of my life was draining far too fast. Now, I savor everything, and each day becomes eternity again!

The Healing Process
Dr. Bonnie McLean

Healing is not an instant fix. True healing needs to occur on all levels: body/mind/emotions/spirit. The healing process is incremental. We make mistakes. Often, these errors are our greatest teachers. Healing takes time and patience with ourselves and one another. We heal best with the support of others. Community can be a powerful healer. We can all heal. It is through our own healing process that we become able to help others do the same.

Love Always Finds a Way
Laura Staley

Listening and trusting my gut, heart, and body every single time—no matter what another person says about me or my life—supports healthier choices. Discontinuing self-blame for the shameful words and deeds of other individuals allows me to connect with and evolve from my Inner Fly on the Wall. I can take the time to flow through hurts in the heart, because the safe passage of emotions continues to be empowering, courageous, and healing work. Movement, meditation, and gratitude practice transform how I experience life. Love always finds a way to love.

Our Powerful Mind
Ken Walls

If I had known thirty years ago how powerful the mind is, I would have saved myself and many others a lot of unnecessary pain. All of the people I met who seemed to just have it "figured out" actually had a formula. It's like baking a cake. If you have the correct ingredients and recipe, it will turn out perfectly every time. The power of writing things down, setting an intention, and meditating is completely immeasurable.

God's Love Broke the Lock
Dr. Anne Worth

For many years, I locked my heart and withheld myself physically and emotionally from those who had hurt me. Try as I might, I couldn't forgive them or myself on my own. God made a way for me to see the hurt through His eyes, and I realized that every person involved was simply a lost and wounded human being. When God's love broke the lock on my heart, forgiveness flowed out to them and me. Now, with God's help, I don't have to let the sun set on my anger.

Penalty Flags
Dr. Mark Heidt

To accomplish any meaningful goal, we must face trials of faith, the purpose of which is to strengthen our resilience and build our character. These trials sharpen our iron and empower us with a laser focus that guides us to our predestined prosperity. I now know to treat frustrations as mere penalty flags—not game-enders. In football, you may lose a few yards, wiping out a momentary gain, but your team gets to run another play. In the quiet and calm, you realize that the penalty flags are each an opportunity to begin again, wiser, and with additional information gained about the opposition, bringing you closer to the goal.

Thank You, God
Teresa Velardi

I've had my share of challenges, but God has given me so much more to look at than those problems. I have seen the love of God, the provision of God, the protection of God, and the power of God come alive in my life. Covered in His unconditional love, I see so clearly now and have such great gratitude in my heart. The awesome God of all creation continues to love and surprise me.

It's a Journey
Kristi Tornabene

If I knew then what I know now, I might have taken control of my health sooner and not had to endure my husband badgering me to lose weight. I would have paid attention to my body as it aged. Proper nutrition would have been something I explored sooner. Realizing I couldn't eat like a teenager and still keep my figure in my aging body, I would have made important changes much sooner and saved some pounds.

AFTERWORD

Laugh 'til it Heals
by Kathleen (Kat) O'Keefe-Kanavos

Laughter takes away the power of whatever holds us prisoner.

As exemplified by the stories in this book, joy is a state of mind, while wellness is a state of being. Laughter can be the glue that binds them. Laughter has always been a form of medicine for me. During my cancer treatment—all three times—I lived by the saying, "Laugh til it heals." Current research agrees. For me, laughter is an innate, God-given gift and weapon.

When nothing else helped during my cancer crisis, I leaned on faith and laughter to find my way to joy and wellness.

Petronelle is a British woman who lived on the corner of High School Street and Main Street in downtown Hyannis on Cape Cod. She was instrumental in teaching me the power of laughter.

"Pete," as she preferred to be called, mentored me during my battle with breast cancer and the writing of my first book, *Surviving Cancerland: Intuitive Aspects of Healing*. Petronelle's pen name was Margot Arnold.

She had written numerous novels filled with exciting espionage and romantic suspense in addition to an acclaimed mystery series.

This amazing woman could always be found sitting on her overstuffed, blue recliner in the living room of the home where she had raised her three children. Now she lived alone. Although the sound of children's squeals of glee was silent, her laughter still echoed off the walls—especially during the nightly news hour, as Petronelle would sit alone in front of her TV set and laugh at the news.

The thing I remember most about Petronelle was her constant joy, which was addictive.

When feeling depressed or frightened, I would call her up and get a "hit of Pete." No matter how bad things appeared, Petronelle discussed the events between peals of laughter. The more dire the situation, the louder her laughter.

Truth be told, at first, I found this behavior quite alarming and questioned her state of mind. However, over time, I realized her approach made any crisis seem less dire, even if it concerned a life-or-death situation or a frightening state of declining health. In her case, it was the loss of her eyesight.

"Yes, my doctor told me I'm going blind," she laughed with a twinkle in her eye. "I'm learning Braille because, although my eyes may fail me, my fingers still work." Then she belly-laughed at her joke and rocked in the blue chair. I stood in the doorway with my mouth open in shocked dismay.

How could anyone living alone laugh about going blind?

But there was something about a crisis delivered with a British accent followed by howling laughter that seemed to make everything so much better.

"Eventually, we are all going to die," Petronelle would chuckle, "so it really doesn't matter anyway, dear, does it?" Petronelle had a point. And it made me smile.

The first time Petronelle laughed while she delivered a dire dose of dread, I thought she had lost her mind. But she was just chasing away the Boogey-man.

She could not change the chaotic situation, but she could change how she perceived, accepted, and ultimately delivered it to others. It was Petronelle's version of Dr. Richard Davidson's research concerning the four skills to strengthen the brain's neural circuits to create joy, which I shared earlier in the Psychology of Joy.[1]

Petronelle handled and conquered fear from the higher vibration of joy and laughter.

Leading by example, she taught me how to laugh in the face of fear. This served me well during my many surgeries and treatments. Following in Petronelle's footsteps, I laughed about anything, or nothing. I dug to find my joy buried beneath the pain. At times, my husband wondered about *my* mental state.

Delivering catastrophic news via laughter chased Petronelle's Blindness Boogey-man and my Cancer Boogey-man right out the front door of life.

Fear cannot live in a laughter-filled environment.

I decided to find out how and why laughter lifted me from the depths of despair. The results of my research during my "crappy" cancer days surprised me.

Something amazing happens to our mind, body, and soul when we laugh. Laughter creates a scientifically measurable, positive change. *Forbes*[2] magazine explained how laughter has an anti-inflammatory effect that protects blood vessels and heart muscles from the damaging effects of cardiovascular disease. A side-effect my doctors watched for during my chemotherapy is heart damage. Hearty laughter became part of my heart disease prevention program. And, according to the Journal of Neuroscience[3], laughter can release potent endorphins, our brain's natural, homegrown, feel-good chemicals, delivered via opioid receptors.

One of the most recent studies on laughter shows that laughing with other people releases endorphins in the brain.[4] The more opioid receptors a given person has in their brain, the more powerful the effect. Our laughter can be our natural and healthy "happy pill."

Petronelle and I were sharing happy pills.

The endorphin effect also explained why, whenever Petronelle laughed at something frightening, I laughed, too. It went beyond two unhinged people giggling like fools.

Social laughter is contagious, and it contagiously forms social bonds.

When an endorphin release spreads through groups, it promotes a sense of togetherness and safety. Each person in the social unit becomes a transmitter of good feelings to others, via laughter. That is why, when someone starts laughing, others will laugh even if they are not sure why everyone is laughing. The reason is not as important as the good feeling of belonging.

This information cemented my decision to start smiling and laughing about anything and everything frightening during my chemo infusions. To my surprise, people would show up beside my infusion chair just to sit with me and giggle.

At first, the concept of laughing in the face of fear felt forced and uncomfortable. However, over time, it replaced my old behavior of becoming anxious and worried. Laughter in the face of danger became a new habit that naturally enhanced my focus for problem-solving.

Whenever someone would ask me, "How can you laugh at a time like this?" I would answer, "Try it. You might like it, and what do you have to lose?"

It was easier for me to see a solution when fear was laughed out of the equation.

One way for me to reach this positive point was to go onto the internet and read jokes and books that transitioned from crisis to joy, or watching old reruns on TV like *I Love Lucy* or *The Three Stooges*. They let me howl with laughter. It felt terrific to become child-like again.

Laughter also improved my emotional and physical well-being, because to laugh, I must take in a deep breath of life. Here is a joke that was so silly, I could not stop giggling.

Q: Where do sick boats go to get healthy?

A: To the dock!

Go ahead and try not to smile.

During crappy times, laughter may be just what the doctor ordered to turn the corner to becoming happy. Like love, laughter cannot be bought, because it is already owned—yet it is priceless. When laughter began to seep into my dreams and nightmares, I knew my new positive-health-habit had taken root.

My beloved mentor Petronelle died with her eyesight. Her vision was poor, but she was not blind. Did the power of laughter keep her crisis at bay? Was the Boogey-man too embarrassed to return and spread more fear?

Petronelle's laughter and lessons still live on in the echoes of my mind. Despite the odds of surviving breast cancer and recurrence three times, I am still alive and laughing in the face of uncertainty. A good, strong laugh can instantly change my day from crappy to happy.

"Laugh at fear and uncertainty? Impossible!" You might say.

Try it. You might like it and discover a new happy-medicine, too.

Joy is the Journey
by Rev. Ariel Patricia

Become comfortable in your uncomfortableness.

I don't know why
babies cry
clouds drift
tears fall
peace is elusive
time passes
hearts break

And I am finally okay with that.

Much of our lives are defined by working.

We work to be successful whether in athletics, the arts, business, relationships, or life in general. When bumps or even major potholes in the road appear—and they will—most of us spring into action… after we dry our tears and pick ourselves up off the floor, that is.

Typically, we will dive deep into work or study to help us figure things out. Understanding the *why* or the *how* helps us to feel in control. We can begin to make sense of our life and circumstance. Much of the time, this work is mainly intellectual. For most of us, this works. Until it doesn't.

The work of the heart.

When life becomes messy, the typical response from our minds no longer works. We need to engage our hearts.

The first time I was told to "move from my head to my heart," my response was "Sounds great. How in the heck do I do that?"

Many years of study, practice, and doing has brought me to the beautiful place of "I don't know." Now, I don't mean I don't know how to do it… it means I know enough to understand that it's okay not to have all the answers. I have become comfortable in my uncomfortableness.

Life is growth.

And growth is change. Resistance is futile. Opening to life, to growth, and to change is the journey. Feeling life, growth, and change is the joy.

May joy become you.

Much love,
Ariel Patricia

ADDITIONAL READING

Chaos to Clarity: Sacred Stories of Transformational Change – November 20, 2019, Sacred Stories Publishing, Kathleen O'Keefe-Kanavos (Co-Author), Rev. Patricia Cagganello (Co-Author), Bernie Siegel M.D. (Foreword), Deborah J. Beauvais, Constance Bramer, Jess Campmans, Tamara Knox, Maria Lehtman, Ellie Pechet, Kristi Tornabene, Teresa Velardi (Contributing Authors)

Dreams That Can Save Your Life: Early Warning Signs of Cancer and Other Diseases – April 17, 2018, Findhorn/Inner Traditions, Larry Burk M.D. C.E.H.P. (Author), Kathleen O'Keefe-Kanavos (Author), Bernie Siegel M.D. (Foreword)

Surviving Cancerland: Intuitive Aspects of Healing – March 28, 2014 Cypress House, Kathleen O'Keefe-Kanavos (Author)

God is in the Little Things: Messages from the Animals – republished June 26, 2016, Sacred Stories Publishing, Patricia Brooks (Author)

God is in the Little Things: Messages from the Golden Angels – republished May 30, 2016, Sacred Stories Publishing, Patricia Brooks (Author)

Scanning for Signal – November 17, 2016, Sacred Stories Publishing, Patricia Brooks (Co-Author)

The Celestine Prophecy – September 18, 2018 (Reissue edition), Grand Central Publishing, James Redfield (Author)

The Tenth Insight: Holding the Vision – December 1, 1998, Grand Central Publishing, James Redfield (Author)

The Secret of Shambhala: In Search of the Eleventh Insight – November 1, 2001, Warner Books, James Redfield (Author)

The Twelfth Insight: The Hour of Decision – February 9, 2012, Grand Central Publishing, James Redfield (Author)

The Right to Be You – 2008, Temple Press, Temple Hayes (Author)

How to Speak Unity – 2010, DeVorss Publishing, Temple Hayes (Author)

When Did You Die? 8 Steps to Stop Dying Every Day and Start Waking Up – 2014, First Edition-HCI Publishing, Second Edition, Amazon Publishing, Temple Hayes (Author)

Love, Medicine & Miracles – 1998, Harper Perennial, Bernie Siegel, MD (Author)

When You Realize How Perfect Everything Is: A Conversation Between Grandfather and Grandson – 2020, Sacred Stories Publishing, Bernie Siegel, MD (Co-Author)

The Art of Healing: Uncovering Your Inner Wisdom and Potential for Self-Healing– 2013, New World Library, Bernie Siegel, MD (Author)

262

No Endings, Only Beginnings: A Doctor's Notes on Living, Loving, and Learning Who You Are – 2020, Hay House, Bernie Siegel, MD (Author)

How Connie Got Her Rack Back: A Breast Cancer Memoir – February 2, 2018, Friesen Press, Constance Bramer (Author)

The She Shift: HiStory to HerStory– June 18, 2018, Melissa Clark, Constance Bramer (Contributing Author)

Pebbles in the Pond: Transforming the World One Person at a Time, Wave Four, Christine Kloser, June 9, 2015, Transformation Books, Tamee Knox (Contributing Author)

Spread Your Wings and Fly: Spiritually Volume 3 – March 2, 2015, Ellie Pechet, M.Ed. (Contributing Author)

Hitching A Ride: A Guide to Earthbound Spirits and How They Affect You, October 1, 2015, Ellie Pechet, M.Ed. (Author)

Final Redemption – March 23, 2017, Sacred Stories Publishing, Helen Heinmiller (Author)

The Rustling of Angels – April 2, 2008, AuthorHouse, Helen Heinmiller (Author)

Going North! Tips & Techniques to Advance Yourself – October 26, 2016, CreateSpace, Dominique B. Brightmon (Author)

Stay the Course: The Elite Performer's 7 Secret Keys to Sustainable Success – May 8, 2019, Dominique B. Brightmon (Author)

Dew Drops – November 27, 2013, Books on Demand, Maria Lehtman (Author)

The Dreaming Doors – May 29, 2018; Books on Demand, Maria Lehtman (Author)

The Truth about IBS and Anxiety: Erasing the Symptoms Effortlessly – November 6, 2019, Diane M. Vich (Author)

Bubble Bee: A Special Story and Meditation for Crisis Support – April 3, 2020, Diane Vich (Author)

A Walk in the Tuscan Sun – March 27, 2019, Veronica Roze (Author)

Every Heart Has a Gift – 2020, Every Heart Project, Catherine Paour (Contributing Author)

When the Wife Cheats – 2010, Frank Zaccari (Author)

From the Ashes: The Rise of the University of Washington Volleyball Program – 2010 Frank Zaccari (Author)

Inside the Spaghetti Bowl – 2011, Frank Zaccari (Co-Author)

Five Years to Live – 2012, Frank Zaccari (Co-Author)

Storm Seeds – 2012, Frank Zaccari (Co-Author)

Empower! Women's Stories of Breakthrough, Discovery and Triumph – Beth Caldwell, 2013, PA Family Publishing, Janet Cincotta (Contributing Author)

30 Days to Me: A Work-ing Book to Living a Serendipitous Life – 2017, Sacred Stories Publishing, Lynn Reilly (Author)

The Secret to Beating the Dragon – 2017, Sacred Stories Publishing, Lynn Reilly (Author)

The Forgiveness Solution: A Step by Step Process to Let It Go – July 11, 2017, Sacred Stories Publishing, Rev. Misty Tyme (Author)

Highest Love – In Sacred Unity with Autoimmunity – June 2020, Expert Insights Publishing. Tamara Knox (Author)

Walls of Wisdom: Turning Pain into Profit – October 2017, Ken Walls (Author)

Integrative Medicine: The Return of the Soul to Healthcare – 2015; Balboa Press, Bonnie McLean OMD (Author)

Live Inspired – April 2020, Sacred Stories Publishing, Laura Staley (Author)

Let Go Courageously and Live with Love: Transform Your Life with Feng Shui – July 2016, Laura Staley (Author)

Cherish Your World Gift Book of 100 Tips to Enhance Your Home and Life – Sept. 2018, Laura Staley (Author)

Call me Worthy: Unlocking a Painful Past for a Glorious Future – 2019, Dr. Anne Worth (Author)

Stories of Roaring Faith – 2019, Dr. Anne Worth (Contributing Author)

One Year Life Verse Devotional –Jay Payleitner, 2007, Tyndale House Publishers, Dr. Anne Worth (Contributing Author)

But Lord, I was Happy Shallow: Lessons Learned in the Deep Places – Marita Littauer, 2004, Kregel Publications, Dr. Anne Worth (Contributing Author)

God Allows U Turns: True Stories of Hope and Healing – Bottke, Hutchings, et al, 2001, Promise Press, Dr. Anne Worth (Contributing Author)

Keys 2 Basic Health: Proactive Strategies for Healthy Aging Especially for Those with MTHFR – March 18, 2020, Kristi Tornabene (Author)

Fractured Grace: How to Create Beauty, Peace and Healing for Yourself and the World – June 2019, Julie Krull (Author)

The Paper Doll Kids – December 2019, Deborah Beauvais (Author)

BOOK CLUB QUESTIONS

1. Are our difficult or painful situations part of a natural learning curve for life? Would we be able to progress spiritually and emotionally without the challenges? Give personal examples that mirror stories in the book.
2. Which story in the book showed you the most progress from a place of Crappy to Happy?
3. Which story in the book was your favorite? Why?
4. Is there a difference between the spiritual and psychological ways you deal with difficult challenges in life?

MEET OUR CONTRIBUTORS

Our Foreword is written by **James Redfield**, author of *The Celestine Prophecy*. Using an adventure parable approach that has been called "part Indiana Jones, part Scott Peck," *The Celestine Prophecy* created a model for spiritual perception and actualization that focused on the mysterious coincidences that occur in each of our lives. The book resonated with millions of people and quickly climbed to the #1 position on the New York Times bestsellers list, remaining on the list for more than two years. Find out more at celestinevision.com

Deborah J. Beauvais is the Founder/Owner of Dreamvisions 7 Radio Network, which was created out of love with a vision to consciously serve humanity. She is an intuitive, healer, and facilitator of Light as a Reconnective Healing™ and The Reconnection™ Practitioner, trained by Dr. Eric Pearl. Deborah is founder of the Kids 4 Love Project and Kids 4 Love Project Radio Show. She is author of *The Paper Doll Kids,* co-written with Janine Ouellette Sullivan. Her syndicated radio show *Love by Intuition* fosters love, healing and unity. dreamvisions7radio.com

Constance (Connie) Bramer is an entrepreneur, mom, breast cancer survivor, and author of *How Connie Got Her Rack Back*, her comical spin on the journey of cancer. Connie's mission to help others through her own experiences drove her to found Get Your Rack Back Inc., a not-for-profit organization that provides financial assistance to cancer patients in Upstate NY. Connie is a Featured Contributor at *BIZCATALYST360* and podcast host of *Laughter and Inspiration with Connie Bramer* on Speaking to the Heart Podcast Network. gyrb.org/about-us/about-connie

Lorilyn Rizzo Bridges is passionate about living life with love, faith, humor, and gratitude. She's a wife, mom, teacher, and writer, and she inspires others to find the beauty and joy in their journey. Lorilyn has overcome some big challenges and shares the wisdom learned in her stories and Instagram page: instagram.com/just.lorilyn/

Dominique Brightmon, DTM is an award-winning speaker, certified leadership trainer, and host of the top-rated *Going North* podcast that features authors from around the world. His mantra is: Advance others to advance yourself. Learn more about him on dombrightmon.com

Jess Campmans is an equine-guided sacred messenger and a bridge between worlds, offering sacred insights and guidance for transforming curses into blessings, mysteries into miracles, and potential into reality through soul recognition and restoration, guided by the universal wisdom of the horse. jesscampmans.com

Janet Cincotta is a graduate of SUNY Upstate Medical Center, a published author, and a physician with more than thirty years of experience in family medicine. She is a contributor to *Empower—Women's Stories of Breakthrough, Discovery and Triumph*. She publishes a weekly blog titled *Storytelling~The Healing Path* at thenarrativepath.blogspot.com

Rev. Dr. Temple Hayes is an author, spiritual leader, and difference-maker. She is the CEO of First Unity Spiritual Campus, which transcends religious denominations, embraces all ethnicity, and reaches beyond national borders. She is also on the leadership team of the Association of Global New Thought and is the founder of illli.org, an online university for lifelong learners and people called to be difference-makers through powerful leadership. templehayes.com

Dr. Mark T. Heidt is a speaker, real estate investor, infomercial producer, Director of the Comedy Hall of Fame, and director of a publicly traded company. He holds a business degree from Syracuse University and a Doctorate of Law degree from Stetson University College of Law. He is currently working on his first book.

Helen Heinmiller is an author and healer who offers transformational light language and color healing techniques to help people of all ages lead healthier and happier lives. Helen is a Featured Contributor at *BIZCATALYST 360°* and author of two spiritual adventure novels, *The Rustling of Angels* and *Final Redemption*. helenheinmiller.com

Tamara Knox Ph.D., PsyThD is an author and devoted admirer of Theocentric Consciousness. She uses food, sound, breath, and movement to access other realms to balance the mind and body, which allows for spiritual cohesiveness. shekhinahpath.com

Dr. Julie Krull is a founding steward of goodofthewhole.com. She hosts *The Dr. Julie Show: All Things Connected* and is the author of the #1 International Bestselling and Nautilus Award-winning book, *Fractured Grace*. juliekrull.com

Maria Lehtman has more than twenty years of experience in the telecommunications and travel industry. She currently works in International Sales & Marketing. Maria specializes in digital photography and writing about digital and self-transformation. She is a columnist for *BIZCATALYST 360°*.

Judy Lemon is a shamanic practitioner and trauma therapist with a private practice in Southern California. She brings her extensive experience and knowledge into her work of helping others to develop their own spiritual gifts. Judy is the author of *Machete Woman – A Tale of Resilience and Rebirth*, which will be published soon. judylemon.com

Bonnie McLean O.M.D., A.P. is a Doctor of Oriental Medicine. With more than fifty years of experience in the healthcare field, she has been named Top Doctor of Oriental Medicine and Acupuncture and Top Holistic Healer of the Decade by I.A.O.T.P., and Top Practitioner of Alternative Medicine in Gulf Breeze, Fl. spiritgatemedicine.com

Catherine Paour is a blogger and storyteller with decades of experience as a perpetual patient. Her courage to share her missed diagnoses with hope, happiness, and humor is both interesting and inspiring. She advocates for trusting your intuition and for medical record accuracy. holeheartedcourage.com

Ellie Pechet, M.Ed. is a metaphysician, medium, shaman, and author with thirty-four years of experience in the intuitive counseling/energy healing field. She works successfully with clients all over the world and heals emotional & physical issues such as grief, depression, trauma, anxiety, chronic pain, and many physical conditions. phoenixrisinghealing.com

Mike Pitocco is married with three children. He retired after thirty-three years with the California Department of Corrections and Rehabilitation as a Program Coordinator in the department's drug treatment initiative. Since then, he has been a chaplain, a consultant with UC San Diego, and Ministry Director for Celebrate Recovery, a faith-based recovery program.

Lynn Reilly is the author of the self-care book *30 Days to Me: A Working Book to Living a Serendipitous Life*. She is a Licensed Professional Counselor and Master Energy Therapist whose passion is educating people on how to understand and support themselves to live a serendipitous life ... a life filled with unexpected joy ... a life meant to be. livingwithserendipity.com

Bernie Siegel, MD has touched many lives all over our planet. In 1978, he began talking about patient empowerment and the choice to live fully and die in peace. As a physician who has cared for and counseled innumerable people and whose own mortality was threatened by illness, Bernie embraces a philosophy of living and dying that stands at the forefront of the medical ethics and spiritual issues with which our society grapples today. He continues to assist in the breaking of new ground in the field of healing and personally struggling to live the message of kindness and love. berniesiegelmd.com

Laura Staley is the author of the book *Live Inspired* and the founder of Cherish Your World. Laura passionately helps people thrive by guiding them to holistic transformations for home, heart, and life. As a columnist, Laura writes personal essays focused on self-discovery, feng shui, emotional health, and transformations from the inside out. cherishyourworld.com loveyourspaceloveyourlife.com

Kristi Tornabene, author of *Keys 2 Basic Health-Proactive Strategies for Healthy Aging* has always been interested in health and well-being. Kristi says, "Without your health, nothing else is possible." keystobasichealth. com

Misty Tyme is a Forgiveness Expert, author, speaker, corporate trainer, host / emcee, Certified Death Doula, Interfaith Reverend, author of the self-help book *The Forgiveness Solution*, and creator of The Forgiveness Algorithm™. Her mission is clear: to bring a forgiveness tool to a cynical world that is craving a way to let go of pain and anger. mistytyme.com

Teresa Velardi is an author, speaker, publisher, and potter. Committed to making a difference in the lives of others, she uses her gifts to help people get their stories told in books. Teresa is currently working on her own book. teresavelardi.com

Diane Vich is a registered nurse, professor, author, and holistic health coach. Her specialty is helping women with chronic pain, digestive issues, and anxiety using alternative approaches to release trauma and pain. Listen to Diane's podcast Goddess Unleashed and download her book and a free meditation. dianevich.com

Ken Walls has taken the tragedies and triumphs of his life and used them to better understand people and know how to help someone overcome, expand, and flourish in their life and in business. He is the author of the

#1 bestselling book *Walls of Wisdom: Turning Pain into Profit*. kenwalls. com

Dr. Anne Worth is a Christian author, speaker, counselor, and workshop leader. She has a heart for animals and people, especially those in need of fostering. Anne serves the homeless and refugee communities in Dallas, Texas. Her mission is to "champion the forgotten." dranneworthauthor. com

Frank Zaccari has written and published five books based on life altering events. Frank teaches a program for entrepreneurs at Arizona State University; he is a mentor with the Veterans Treatment Court; a mentor and judge with the University of California Entrepreneurship Academy; the host of a weekly radio show Life Altering Events; and is an accomplished speaker. frankzaccari.com

MEET OUR AUTHORS

Rev. Ariel Patricia is CEO and Founder of Sacred Stories Media, a conscious online media network. Sacred Stories Media includes Sacred Stories Publishing, an award-winning traditional book publishing and marketing company; Garnet Press, a self-publishing book division; and Sacred U, an online course division.

As an ordained interfaith, interspiritual minister, Ariel Patricia believes every story is a sacred story. She is ordained from One Spirit Interfaith Seminary in New York and has earned her Master of Arts in Education and her Bachelor of Science in Business. Ariel Patricia worked in the corporate and educational worlds for many years and proudly served six years as a sergeant in the U.S. Marine Corps.

Ariel Patricia is the author of two books sharing the beginning of her spiritual journey— *God is in the Little Things: Messages from the Animals* and *God is in the Little Things: Messages from the Golden Angels*—and is co-author of a poetry book, *Scanning For Signal*, and co-author of the first book of the Sacred Stories of Transformation series: *Chaos to Clarity: Sacred Stories of Transformational Change.*

Learn more at:

sacredstoriesmedia.com and sacredstoriespublishing.com

Kathleen (Kat) O'Keefe-Kanavos is accredited in Psychopathology and Special Education. Kat taught Psychology at USF, Ft. Myers Branch, and taught the severely emotionally handicapped for ten years. She served as Special Education Department Head for two years before retiring.

Kat is also known as The Queen of Dreams in her internationally syndicated columns, *PR Guru*, and video podcaster/radio show host on DreamVisions7 Radio Network, *Dreaming Healing*. Kat is a three-time breast cancer survivor whose dreams diagnosed her illness, which was missed by the medical community and the tests on which they relied. Kat says, "My dreams and my doctors saved my life." She is also a multi-award-winning author and Dream Expert who has been seen on Dr. Oz, Doctors, NBC, and CBS. Kat and Duke University Radiologist Dr. Larry Burk co-wrote the 2018 Nautilus Award Winner, *Dreams That Can Save Your Life*. She is currently working on a co-authored series with Rev. Ariel Patricia of Sacred Stories Publishing. As a content editor, Kat helps authors with the organizing and writing of their books.

Kat's an international author/lecturer and keynote speaker who promotes patient advocacy and connecting with Divine-guidance through Dreams for success in health, wealth, and relationships. "Don't tell God how big your problems are. Tell your problems how big your God is."

Learn more at kathleenokeefekanavos.com

ENDNOTES

Psychology of Joy

References:

1. Why we cry - American Psychological Association. https://www.apa.org/monitor/2014/02/cry

2. Why Joy Is Better Than Happiness - The Atlantic. https://www.theatlantic.com/health/archive/2019/06/why-joy-better-happiness/592735/

3. Laugh for Longevity! – New Research on Laughter and COVID https://www.bizcatalyst360.com/laugh-for-longevity-new-research-on-laughter-and-covid-19/

4. New Laughter Research and COVID-19: Laugh for Longevity! https://www.patheos.com/blogs/aboveandbeyondthe5senses/2020/03/new-laughter-research-and-covid-19-laugh-for-longevity/

5. Study: Laughter Really Is Contagious | Live Science. https://www.livescience.com/9430-study-laughter-contagious.html

6. Richard Davidson, Wikipedia. https://en.wikipedia.org/wiki/Richard_J._Davidson

7. The Four Keys to Well-Being | Greater Good. https://greatergood.berkeley.edu/article/item/the_four_keys_to_well_being

Part 1 Final Thoughts

1. Evolution Counseling https://evolutioncounseling.com/love-is-a-state-of-being/

2. Science Daily https://www.sciencedaily.com/releases/2020/02/200212150134.htm

Part 2 Final Thoughts
1. Psychology Today https://www.psychologytoday.com/us/blog/the-other-side/201706/in-pursuit-happiness-why-pain-helps-us-feel-pleasure

Part 3 Final Thoughts
1. Conscious Dying Institute https://www.consciousdyinginstitute.com/inspiring-quotes/2017/8/3/death-is-a-rite-of-passage-grief-is-an-initiation-to-new-life

Part 4 Final Thoughts
1. APS Association for Psychological Science- Serious Research on Happiness https://www.psychologicalscience.org/observer/serious-research-on-happiness

Laugh til it Heals

References:
1. The Four Keys to Well-Being | Greater Good. https://greatergood.berkeley.edu/article/item/the_four_keys_to_well_being
2. Six Science-Based Reasons Why Laughter Is The Best Medicine. https://www.forbes.com/sites/daviddisalvo/2017/06/05/six-science-based-reasons-why-laughter-is-the-best-medicine
3. Social Laughter Triggers Endogenous Opioid Release in Humans; Journal of Neuroscience 21 June 2017, 37 (25) 6125-6131; DOI: https://doi.org/10.1523/JNEUROSCI.0688-16.2017   https://www.jneurosci.org/content/37/25/6125